Creative Endurance

56 Rules for Overcoming Obstacles and Achieving Your Goals

MIKE SCHNAIDT

FOREWORD BY STEPHANIE MEHTA

—

ILLUSTRATIONS BY KAGAN McLEOD AND
MARCO GORAN ROMANO

ROCKPORT

QUARTO.COM

© 2024 Quarto Publishing Group USA Inc.

Text © 2024 Mike Schnaidt

First published in 2024 by Rockport Publishers, an imprint of The Quarto Group,

100 Cummings Center, Suite 265-D, Beverly, MA 01915, USA.

T (978) 282-9590
F (978) 283-2742

10 9 8 7 6 5 4 3 2 1

ISBN: 978-0-7603-8482-4

Digital edition published in 2024

eISBN: 978-0-7603-8483-1

Library of Congress Cataloging-in-Publication Data available

Printed in China

▶ **Rockport Publishers** titles are also available at discount for retail, wholesale, promotional, and bulk purchase. For details, contact the Special Sales Manager by email at specialsales@quarto.com or by mail at The Quarto Group, Attn: Special Sales Manager, 100 Cummings Center, Suite 265-D, Beverly, MA 01915, USA.

ART DIRECTION AND DESIGN
Mike Schnaidt

ILLUSTRATIONS
Kagan McLeod (portraits) and Marco Goran Romano (concepts)

TYPEFACES
Circular, Noe, and Sharp Grotesk

"

You need to figure out what
you're really
passionate about, and do it."

—SAGI HAVIV
P.59

"

Sometimes the hill is easy;
sometimes it's steep. But when you
reach the top, all is forgiven."

—YUKO SHIMIZU
P.33

—

This book is dedicated to my students,
past, present, and future. You continue to inspire me,
and I hope this book inspires you.

Contents

14

YOUR DAY

50

YOUR PROJECT

86

YOUR JOB

122

YOUR LIFE

Foreword

—

BY STEPHANIE MEHTA

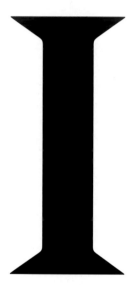

IT'S AN EXCITING TIME TO BE A CREATIVE. Interest in creativity and the creative process has perhaps never been greater. Management consulting firm McKinsey, best known for helping companies maximize profits, has started issuing reports linking creativity value and financial performance. *Fast Company* issues an annual list of the Most Creative People in Business, celebrating artists, inventors, designers, and corporate executives who deploy innovation and unconventional thinking to solve big problems. Start-ups and established brands alike are starting to appoint creative directors to burnish their credibility with younger consumers.

Few people advocate for creativity in business like Brian Chesky, the cofounder and CEO of Airbnb. A graduate of the Rhode Island School of Design, Chesky calls Airbnb an "entirely creatively led company," and he's urged corporate leaders to consider adding creative folks to their boards of directors. Creativity "should be in the [board]room. It should be in the conversation," he says.

But even as the business community professes ardor for creativity, most corporate executives don't actually know how to harness it. Fewer than half of design leaders surveyed by McKinsey say their CEOs fully understand their role, and only one in ten CEOs say their senior designer is involved in strategy. The report concludes that many chief designers are doomed to fail because they lack the authority to make the meaningful creative contributions they were hired to bring to the organization.

And research from ad agency TBWA Worldwide finds creative talent are more likely to feel "burned out or discouraged" than the overall workforce.

▶ **Stephanie Mehta** is the CEO and chief content officer of Mansueto Ventures, the parent company of *Fast Company* and *Inc.*

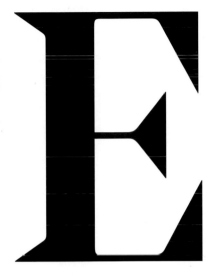

ENTER CREATIVE ENDURANCE.
Mike Schnaidt offers practical, digestible tips to help reenergize creatives—and just about anyone else who is feeling a bit blocked. Many of the contributors are professional athletes or creative leaders who previously played competitive sports, and their stories about overcoming adversity and challenges give the book energy and urgency that you won't find in other books on creativity, which can be a little on the contemplative side.

I met Mike in 2018, when I was recruiting a creative director for *Fast Company*. Because *Fast Company* assertively covers design, I was seeking a partner who would elevate the look and feel of our magazine, website, and events to give us credibility with the creative community—but not push the design so far that we'd alienate more traditional business readers. I came armed with all sorts of questions aimed at teasing out Mike's point of view and influences. We talked about creative

" THE STORIES ABOUT OVERCOMING ADVERSITY AND CHALLENGES GIVE THIS BOOK ENERGY AND URGENCY THAT YOU WON'T FIND IN OTHER BOOKS ON CREATIVITY. "

directors we admired, photography, tight budgets, and who *Fast Company*'s readers are. It was only when I left our first meeting that I realized that he'd interviewed me. He got the job and brought that same level of inquiry to his role: He's known to ask lots of questions to understand the underlying philosophy and themes of the work he's about to tackle.

Lucky reader, you are the beneficiary of Mike's insatiable curiosity. The twenty subjects featured in the book represent just a portion of the people he interviewed and consulted for this project.

Imagine Mike's delight when he realized that researching this book would entail calling up a bunch of people he admires and asking for their insights on creativity, perseverance, and more. And it is a testament to Mike's big-hearted world view that his subjects truly come from all backgrounds and walks of life. I can't think of many other books about creativity that include interviews with a nine-year-old and a seventy six year old, a Black woman astronaut *and* a bank vice president.

I've also observed Mike's own brand of creative endurance up close. He really practices what he preaches in the book, and creatives will glean some smart insights on how to deal with executives who say they want creativity but can't always articulate their intentions. (Yeah, that would be me.) Noncreatives should read it, too. Not only will you learn what your creative counterparts do all day, you'll quickly realize they've got the creativity—and with Mike's help, the endurance—to help you solve all manner of challenges.

Introduction

—

BY MIKE SCHNAIDT

IF IT WEREN'T FOR RUNNING, I wouldn't be as creative as I am today.

It's mile sixteen of the New York City Marathon on a hot November day. As I stride across the Queensboro Bridge, something feels...*off*. I'm sweating profusely. Muscle cramps squeeze my calves, hamstrings, and quadriceps into a vice. My right forearm locks into a forty-five-degree angle. I look like the Tin Man trying to run a potato sack race.

Curse the weather gods for sucker-punching me with this heat. *Did I just sweat all my electrolytes out?*

The cramps worsen with each step forward. One thing becomes crystal clear: My personal goal of a time juuust a little bit faster than four hours and twenty-two minutes (my previous marathon time), has been blown to bits—thanks to these muscle cramps. I'm frozen in place.

As the other runners bolt past, I slow my mind and let my thoughts simmer.

This isn't a race against them. This is me against me. If I can overcome this obstacle, I can raise the bar for what I'm capable of.

This tenet provides my body with just enough of a trickle charge to trundle toward the finish line, clocking in at five hours and thirty-two minutes. Not the time I was aiming for, but a huge mental win for me. This reframing tool is known to psychologists as cognitive reappraisal, and it's the key to my creative endurance.

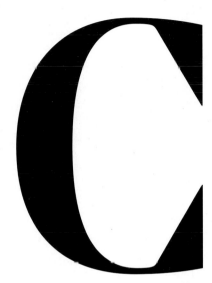

COGNITIVE REAPPRAISAL IS A technique used to reframe a negative situation into a positive one. A tool commonly used by therapists to help patients deal with stress and anxiety, it's applicable to your career as a creative.

Whether you're a designer, writer, photographer, or any other type of creative, your career is full of obstacles. Confusing feedback, tough clients, and slashed budgets are as fun as a cramp in your calf, and they sideline you from making something great. But with cognitive reappraisal, you can reframe those obstacles as creative opportunities. For example, if my budget is tight at *Fast Company*, I'll save money by deploying a typographic solution instead of hiring an outside artist.

Creative Endurance will teach you how to reframe your problems and make better work as a result. Jot this down: A positive response to a problem will create a positive outcome.

GLOSSARY

CREATIVE

Individuals who can generate original ideas or solve problems in new ways. They have the ability to draw connections between seemingly unrelated phenomena. Fields include the arts, science, technology, and business.

ENDURANCE

The ability to exert oneself over an extended period of time. Physical examples include a marathoner, cyclist, or swimmer. In mental terms, it can include a painter who can spend hours in their studio or a writer who works on a book for years.

CREATIVE

ENDURANCE

The persistence through challenges and obstacles that occur throughout the creative process. Creative endurance involves the development of resilience, optimism, and grit to overcome these challenges. Read about those tools on the next page.

HERE'S A BRIEF OVERVIEW OF THE BOOK

SECTION 1: YOUR DAY

In this section, you'll learn how to overcome obstacles in your daily routine. You'll build focus, race through distractions, be imaginative in boring meetings, and develop a sustainable creative practice.

SECTION 2: YOUR PROJECT

Here, you'll hone your creative process through proven techniques for brainstorming, researching, and prototyping. You'll gain skills in selling your ideas to clients and employing their feedback.

SECTION 3: YOUR JOB

This section will guide you through the creative industry with practical tactics for interviewing, hiring, and *gulp* getting fired. You'll also learn about creative budgeting and presentations. Fun!

SECTION 4: YOUR LIFE

Finally, you enter the big-picture phase of your career. This section will help you discover your creative voice, personal values, and long-term goals for making an impact in your industry.

EACH SECTION ENDS WITH actionable takeaways and activities. The book is designed to be easily digestible, with stories no longer than two pages.

Whether you're running a race or tackling a big project at work, overcoming an obstacle will always be rewarding. While your career may feel like a marathon, with the tools and strategies in this book, you won't have to suffer.

Grit

Ultramarathoner Dean Karnazes ran across the United States over the course of fifty days, but on day nineteen, he hit his wall halfway through a marathon in Arizona. To overcome this obstacle, he focused on the present and broke the race down into a series of smaller steps. Karnazes explains, "It's a Zen-like experience and helps me get through anything." This strategy helped him through the remainder of the race and can be applied to any big project in your career. By breaking the project down into a series of manageable steps, you avoid feeling overwhelmed and increase your chances of success. Read about Karnazes on page 36.

PACK THESE TOOLS

THREE MENTAL CHARACTERISTICS FOR CREATIVE SUCCESS.

Resilie

WITH THE UNDERSTANDING THAT cognitive reappraisal is the driveshaft that turns obstacles into opportunities, it's time to open up your toolbox. You have a trio of tools: resilience, grit, and optimism. Resilience rebounds you from setbacks, grit empowers you to persevere through hardship, and optimism fuels your confidence to achieve your goals. In this book, you'll encounter stories from a diverse range of professionals who've faced their own obstacles, such as self-doubt, failure, and lack of inspiration. Through their experiences, you'll discover inspiration and insight to apply to your career.

The astronaut Jeanette Epps has dreamed of going to space since she was a child. In 2018, her trip to the International Space Station was put on pause for undisclosed reasons. "Things won't always go as planned," she says. Epps remains optimistic and believes "the journey is the creative part." Epps's story on page 26 will give you a boost of inspiration.

Graphic designer Sagi Haviv is the definition of resilience. When he first came to the United States from Israel, he didn't make it into Cooper Union, the prestigious art school. He trained as a method actor for a year to secure his visa and was accepted to Cooper Union on his second shot. Years later, when Haviv applied to Chermayeff & Geismar, they didn't have any openings. He demonstrated his passion by offering to work for free. Today, he's a partner at Chermayeff & Geismar & Haviv, where he designs brands for some of the biggest companies in the world, including the U.S. Open and Conservation International. His inspiring story of resilience begins on page 58.

nce

Optimism

Who's Who

THE ARTISTS, ATHLETES, AND EVERYONE IN BETWEEN THE PAGES OF THIS BOOK.

RUI ABREU
Portugal-based type designer and founder of R-Typography. Abreu's craft of type design is meticulous and monotonous—and requires a unique type of endurance.

MASSY ARIAS
Fitness influencer and entrepreneur, featured on the cover of magazines such as *Women's Health* and *Parents Latina*. Single mom, unstoppable work ethic.

MOLLY BAZ
Chef, author of two cookbooks, and video host. I was curious to learn how she remains cool and confident while on camera.

DICK BEARDSLEY
Motivational speaker and former long-distance runner who came in second place to Alberto Salazar in the 1982 Boston Marathon.

EVE BINDER
Design leader in the tech industry. Résumé includes Chase, Grubhub, AOL, and oh, also happens to be my wife.

JEANIE CHEEK
Wardrobe stylist and costume designer who's kept her cool while working on high-pressure television shows such as *Lip Sync Battle* and *MTV Movie Awards*.

DAVID COOPER
The guy who illustrated two children's books for Kevin Hart. What was *that* like?

DAVID CURCURITO
Founder of Works Well With Others Design Group and former design director of *Esquire*, where he was my boss.

BILLY DEMONG
Former Nordic combined skier and five-time Olympian. I wanted to learn more about the mental strength necessary to be an Olympic athlete.

MARION DEUCHARS
Illustrator, graphic designer, and author of twenty books. Utilizes breathing, stretching, and yoga for balance in her workday.

EVELYN DONG
Professional mountain biker who jumps her bike 15 feet (4 m) in the air.

MICHELLE DOUGHERTY
Creative director who oversaw the design for the *Stranger Things* title sequence.

JEANETTE EPPS
NASA astronaut and aerospace engineer. I was curious about the endurance required to be an astronaut.

KARIN FONG
Director of Imaginary Forces, a motion graphics studio responsible for title sequences on everything from *Thursday Night Football* to *Spider-Man*.

RUSSELL FRANCIS
A 76-year-old painter and poet who discovered his creativity later in life.

VINCE FROST
Australian-based graphic designer and founder of Frost*collective design agency.

NOAH GALLOWAY
Former US Army soldier who lost his left arm and leg in Iraq. The definition of grit, Galloway perseveres as an extreme athlete.

CAROLINE GLEICH
Hikes up mountains and skis down them. How does Gleich weather-proof her mind from the imminent danger of avalanches?

CAMILLE GERKE
Third-grade student. I wanted to experience a child's imagination before it's impeded by the practicality of the workplace.

ANTHONY GIGLIO
Sommelier, author, and hilarious public speaker. Humor is a powerful tool for overcoming obstacles.

SAGI HAVIV
Partner at Chermayeff & Geismar & Haviv. I wanted to learn about the struggle with high-profile clients such as the U.S. Open.

HURLEY HAYWOOD
Former race car driver and five-time winner of the 24 Hours of Daytona. Figured a guy who could stay up and drive for an entire day would have a few things to say about endurance.

DEAN KARNAZES
Ultramarathoner who once ran for three days without sleep and has written five books.

JENNIFER KINON
Political campaigns are notoriously tough design sprints, and Kinon was the design director for Hillary Clinton's campaign.

SARA LIEBERMAN
Quit a full-time job in New York to pursue her dream as a Paris-based travel and food writer.

VAISHNAVI MAHENDRAN
Culture is creative fuel for this South Asian art director, currently at Apple Worldwide Retail.

BOBBY C. MARTIN JR.
Creative director at Apple. Scored a dream job working on Cory Booker's political campaign while at Champions Design.

MICHAEL BRANDON MYERS
Myers is an early adopter of AI, and I wanted to learn more about the tool that frightens many creatives.

JAY OSGERBY
Industrial designer responsible for the Pacific chair, which was the seat of choice for Apple Park (the corporate headquarters of Apple).

ALEX PIRANI
Former chef who pivoted in his thirties and went back to school to become a graphic designer. Career changes like these can fuel your endurance by challenging your creativity.

ZAKIYA POPE
Senior behavioral designer and vice president at U.S. Bank. Pope was a successful college volleyball player, and I was intrigued how the sport influenced her views on diversity and design.

JOSHUA RAMUS
Architect who rowed crew while in college. What are the similarities between rowing and architecture?

ANGELA RIECHERS
Transitioned between three careers as a writer, art director, and now program director of graphic design at the University of the Arts.

JASPAL RIYAIT
Once a senior editor at *The New York Times*, now an art director at Apple. Riyait forges her resilience by switching jobs once she's hit peak success.

LEO RODGERS
Cyclist who lost his left leg in a motorcycle accident. Optimistically believes we all "need to get our one crash out of the way." What can we learn from Rodgers about dealing with our own "crashes"?

KEIVARAE RUSSELL
American football cornerback who was once signed by the New Orleans Saints. I wanted to learn how Russell deals with the uncertainty of now being a free agent.

YUKO SHIMIZU
Japanese illustrator and professor at the School of Visual Arts. Shimizu's artwork is elaborate, her work ethic, persistent.

NEIL STRAUSS
I wanted to learn interview techniques from this *New York Times* best-selling writer who's interviewed everyone from Chuck Berry to Lady Gaga.

PETER YANG
What was it like for this celebrity photographer to be on set with Barack Obama?

Day

OVERCOME CREATIVE BLOCKS AND BUILD A SUSTAINABLE PROFESSIONAL PRACTICE.

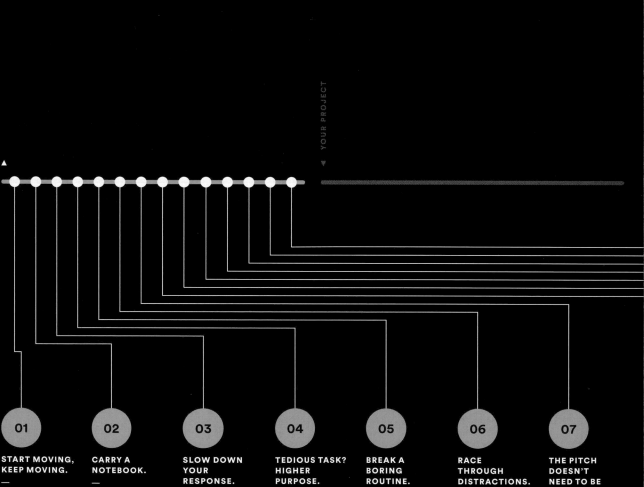

▼ YOUR PROJECT

01

02

03

04

05

06

07

START MOVING,
KEEP MOVING.
—

CARRY A
NOTEBOOK.
—

SLOW DOWN
YOUR
RESPONSE.

TEDIOUS TASK?
HIGHER
PURPOSE.

BREAK A
BORING
ROUTINE.

RACE
THROUGH
DISTRACTIONS.

THE PITCH
DOESN'T
NEED TO BE

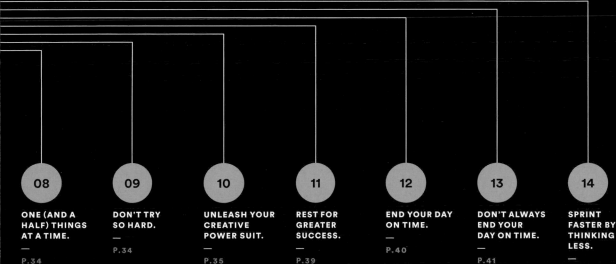

"It's important for my creativity to

not always think of the endgame."

—MOLLY BAZ

▼

P.22

▼

Jay Osgerby, on Being Creative
"I can't resist the excitement of making things, especially with people who are passionate—that feeling is contagious."

START MOVING, KEEP MOVING.

No.

01

Squeeze those
bad jitters into good
creative juice.

IT'S RARE FOR AN ultramarathoner to be stuck in place, but that's exactly where Dean Karnazes finds himself right now. Hovering over his butcher-block writing table, he struggles with the opening scene of his first screenplay. How can he make a film about ancient Greece feel relevant to a modern audience? The problem nags at Karnazes like a splinter jammed under his fingernail.

This scenario of creative paralysis may sound familiar, whether you're struggling to get out of bed, stewing over a difficult project, or overwhelmed by a deadline. Remain still and your anxiety will continue to climb. The solution is simple: "Motion stirs emotion," says Karnazes.

He puts his personal credo into action and embarks upon a head-clearing run. At the 2,600-foot (792 m) summit of Mount Tamalpais, the idea hits Karnazes like a rock rolling down the hill. The film will open with students griping about their first day of Greek Classics Studies. When the professor instructs them to open their books, the film will cut to a battle scene in Athens.

Karnazes returns to his desk to write the opening scene. "The hardest part is finding the inner discipline and motivation to do something that you're not looking forward to," he says.

In this section, you'll meet other heroes who use movement to overcome obstacles. Race car driver Hurley Haywood swiftly cuts through distractions, astronaut Jeanette Epps deliberately multitasks, and mountain biker Evelyn Dong knows when to stop moving at the end of the day.

Carry a Notebook.

—

As you zip through your day, random ideas will flint like fireflies in your brain. Heed the advice of illustrator Marion Deuchars, and keep a notebook handy to jar those sparks of genius. "It's important to get an idea down on paper before I forget it," she says. The author of *Yoga for Stiff Birds* and nineteen other books has discovered forgotten book concepts in her notebook. Bonus: The notebook off-loads your short-term memory, making room for fresh ideas.

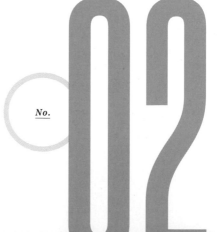

No.

02

↓

PING! A PARANORMAL message pops up, late in the day. "Hey, I forgot, can you create one more graphic," asks your coworker. *Seriously?*

Astronaut Jeanette Epps deals with her fair share of aggravating messages while working at NASA Mission Control as Capcom. In that role, Epps gathers the thoughts of every console in the room, consults with the flight director, and relays critical information back to space.

"Sit back, and think about it. Don't be reactive," she says. "Find out what the real story is." If Capcom mucks up their communication with an astronaut in distress, that could make matters worse.

Whether you're Capcom or creative, your initial response will set the tone. Annoyed at your coworker's message? Don't respond when you're angry. Simple as that. Let the request sit for a bit, and your perception will change. In the morning, it might not feel that annoying.

Even better: Wait, and your coworker might realize they don't actually need that extra graphic.

Look at the situation from the perspective of your coworker. Do they really need that graphic tonight, or are they just knocking an item off their to-do list? *C'mon, that's understandable.*

Let's say the coworker does indeed need that graphic, and these late requests are common. Resolve this situation, but acknowledge the bigger picture:

How an astronaut deals with an onslaught of messages.

Sloooo

There might be a workflow issue. Are you discussing all of the graphic needs at the outset of a project? Is there someone else making these requests, and do they need to be part of the communication from the beginning? Spend some additional time collecting your thoughts, then set up a meeting to discuss these issues.

Talk about problems: When Epps and I spoke, NASA just experienced a coolant leak on the Russian Soyuz rocket. "It's better to laugh than cry in these situations. So much can go wrong—as long as it's not the worst-case scenario, then all is good," she says.

See the bright side like Epps. Last night, the message felt like a crash landing. This morning, it's a chance for liftoff.

No. 03

OOOOW

DOWN YOUR RESPONSE.

 MY GROWTH PLAN

"I don't wake up hungry."

—

MOLLY BAZ SHARES HER RECIPE FOR DAILY INSPIRATION.

OCCUPATION
Cookbook Author,
Video Host

LOCATION
Los Angeles,
California

EXERCISE PRIMES my creative process. I need to feel the urge for food to get really excited to cook. There's nothing worse than feeling full from a meal you just ate and then stepping into the kitchen to create. Nothing happens.

—

THERE ARE TOOLS I use for inspiration. I'll cook in an improvisational way. It's important for my creativity to not always think of the endgame.

—

I MADE CHILI RECENTLY. I sat with my husband, turned on the fireplace, and was like, *We're going all-in on vibes tonight.* He's a big sounding board for me. He will say, "This is yummy. I'm enjoying this, but it's missing a little bit of Molly." When he says that, I'm like, "Ugh, I knew it."

—

MY IDEAS ARE OFTEN shaped through

conversation. My inner and outer thoughts are not always the same, and talking to someone else will help me understand what I *actually* mean.

—

CHILI IS A GREAT EXAMPLE of a recipe that comes from being like, *Oh, that's what I want to eat tonight.* And then, the next day being like, *That was really good. I'm gonna turn that into a recipe.* That chili became Spiced Chili with Many Beans and Some Greens. It's in my cooking club.

—

I USE THE SAME ingredients in multiple ways in a recipe. It's an incredible way to keep ingredient lists tight. On my chili, I started by sautéing onions into the base and reserved a quarter of the onion. I thinly sliced it, tossed it with lime juice, and put pickled onions on top.

—

WHEN CLARKSON POTTER reached out to me to write a cookbook, I was shocked. But they wanted me to write it for Basically, a sub-brand of *Bon Appétit.* After I thought about it, my first book isn't going to be Molly for someone else. It's going to be Molly for Molly.

—

I WAS ASKED TO WRITE a list of one hundred recipe titles as part of my proposal. I started throwing titles on paper, like Pastrami Roast Chicken with Schmaltzy Onions and Dill. Smooshed and Crispy Potatoes with Salt and Vinegar Sour Cream. Things that sounded good to me.

—

NAMING IS IMPORTANT. You have five to six words to explain everything about a dish, from ingredients to technique. You have to be choosy.

—

ONCE THE PROPOSAL was approved, I stepped into the kitchen to tackle those recipes, and the inspiration wasn't there.

TAKEAWAYS

1
Set your ideal environment to be creative. Exercise whets this chef's appetite to write recipes.

2
Don't worry about the end result. Enjoy the process and you'll get there.

3
The act of creating is an evolution. First make it good, then make it great.

MY COOKBOOK RECIPES evolved from the original ideas. Even the kinds of ingredients that I was fixated on changed over time. Every month, there was a new thing I was obsessed with. They find their way into the recipes. Right now, I'm in my sesame seed phase.

—

A RECIPE STARTS WITH A VISUAL in my head   what will the finished dish look like? Taste is important, too, obviously. The two need to intersect to make a recipe great.

—

I MADE A CONSCIOUS DECISION to spend my own money on hiring an outside firm to design the second cookbook. I specifically chose people who are not cookbook designers—I didn't want them to take a traditional approach.

—

GRAPHIC DESIGN and recipes are similar. On the final dish, ingredients need to be balanced. You can't have too much of one thing—it'll overpower the dish.

—

I WAS A LINE COOK. If you get an order in, you have seven minutes to get it out. It's all about efficiency. That eliminates mental chaos.

—

WHEN IT CAME to the techniques in the book, I decided to hold my reader's hand in a way that's not the common convention for recipe writing. I organized the ingredients by the department where you find them in the grocery store. It's annoying when there are herbs on four different parts of the list. You end up running circles around the grocery store.

—

I'M DOING THE THING I'm meant to be doing—teaching people how to cook and having fun while doing it.

▼
**Yuko Shimizu,
on Joy and Purpose**
*"Making something from nothing
is pure joy for creators like
me. Illustration is my purpose,
and it makes me happy."*

Tedious Task?
Higher Purpose.

This Olympic Gold medalist's simple secret for plowing through the mundane.

BILLY DEMONG IS TRAINING FOR THE Nordic combined skiing event in the Olympics. Running for hours on a treadmill, he stares at a Post-it Note with a dot drawn smack in the middle of it. This is a tedious yet meaningful task.

As Demong explains, "Boring is part of the pathway to success." On the treadmill, he's honing his ability to tune out distractions and focus—a crucial skill for thundering down the ski slope.

Demong's strategy is to overprepare. While he's running on the treadmill for hours, the actual Olympic event will entail 30 minutes of cross-country skiing. Less time if he wants to win.

This philosophy applies to creatives as well. Let's say your boss asks you to organize some jpeg files. Boring task, but you can make it meaningful. Remain optimistic: This can lead to something bigger—the opportunity is in your hands. Develop a new workflow for organizing jpegs. Find a new tool. Once you're done, ask your boss if you can work on a larger project. Go above and beyond on boring tasks, and they can take you to your next role.

Put this on a Post-it note: Demong won Olympic Gold in 2010 when he crossed the finish line in 25 minutes, 32.9 seconds. This was a first for the United States in the sport of Nordic combined skiing. All those hours of training led him to success.

No.

EASY
ENDURANCE
BOOST

**GET UP AND
STRETCH**
"When you're sitting and creating, your brain is excited, but your body is suffering," says the illustrator Marion Deuchars. She has two stretches. The Superman: Stretch your arms straight up. The Lobster: Stretch your arms to the side, and bend at the elbow with your fingers aimed at the sky. Hold both for three breaths.

No.

Break a Boring Routine.

One little change a day will make for a big creative slay.

DEAN KARNAZES PEELED OFF HIS PANTS and went for a run.

On his thirtieth birthday, Karnazes stepped outside for a moment of reflection. "I was so comfortable that I was miserable," he says. "Everything came easy, and running was tough." After too many tequila shots, he made the creative decision to run 30 miles (48 km) in celebration of his thirty years on earth. In a pair of silk boxers. On this fateful night, Karnazes discovered his creative approach to breaking routines and quit his cushy corporate job the next day.

We face a similar conundrum to Karnazes: Our minds love routine and hate the struggle that comes with change. As you get better at a creative act, your mind forms the process into a routine—a go-kart track that loops round and round, day in and day out. If you're a fiction writer, that might mean waking up at 5 a.m. every day and grinding out two hours of work. This is when your work gets stale.

Flee out of your comfort zone. Once a week, try writing nonfiction at a local coffee shop, and start at noon. You'll remix your brain patterns and develop a fresh perspective on writing fiction.

Karnazes's birthday jog unlocked his running superpower. During a run across all fifty states, Karnazes was invited to the White House by Michelle Obama. "It was an unbelievable high point," he says. "The White House was the last place on earth I ever thought I'd end up."

Challenge yourself to break a routine today. It might lead to an unexpected tomorrow.

NEW HABITS, MORE CREATIVITY

Flip a few routines for a fresh perspective.

SCHEDULE
If your days feel stale, start earlier, or later. "I never run at the same time two days in a row," says Dean Karnazes about his ultramarathon training. Just check with your boss.

TOOLS
Change your software for a fresh perspective. If I'm stumped while writing on the computer, doodling on a piece of paper will break through any creative blockages.

TIME
Limit yourself to twenty minutes, and it'll reduce the amount of over-thinking. "The idea happens when you don't think about it," says Vince Frost, founder of Frost*collective.

COLLABORATOR
They can point out things you missed—helpful when you're in a time crunch. My wife, Eve, is a designer, and she'll frame feedback based on what's best for a user.

LOCATION
Illustrator Marion Deuchars will go to a noisy coffee shop to focus for an hour. "I find the distraction quite stimulating," she says. "It sets a time and place to focus on one idea."

THE ASTRONAUT

YOU'RE FACING A CREATIVE BLOCK AND **JEANETTE EPPS** IS FLYING AT SUPERSONIC SPEED. HERE'S HOW TO KEEP YOUR COOL.

LOCATION
Houston,
Texas

▼

BEING AN ASTRONAUT IS ONE OF THE coolest jobs on another planet—a dream shared by many but pursued by few. I huddled with Jeanette Epps to learn more about why she wanted to become an astronaut, how she got there, and the challenges she faced in her quest to go to space. I was impressed by her calm demeanor, which she attributes to her time in Iraq. "The real you comes out when you're under pressure," she said. Read on to learn how you can be invincible to stress like this astronaut.

How is being an astronaut creative? When I was a kid, my twin sister and I had this game where we'd watch the Moon follow us home. I was being creative by thinking of the endless possibilities in life. To be an astronaut, you have to dream. *What would it be like to get a little closer to the Moon? Closer to Mars?* Some astronauts come back from space and say it's the blackest black you've ever seen. That's so exciting to me.

You were supposed to go to space, but that didn't happen. How did you deal? I'm an optimist. I always have been. I just had leadership training, and we learned about Crucible Moments: situations that force the real you to come out. How you react to a tough situation is important. When I was removed from the flight, I had to decide who I was at that moment. Resilience is important, in any field you work in. Things won't go as planned. You need to be able to recover fast and properly. In leadership training, we reflected back on our entire life to examine for crucible moments that shaped us.

Did you have a crucible moment as a child?
Hours before my twin sister and I were born, my mother's home was broken into. From that point on, she was always afraid, so we were very protected. We read and studied a lot. Public television was big in my house: *Mister Rogers, Sesame Street, The Electric Company,* and *Vegetable Soup.* That crucible moment shaded my mother's life and the ways she raised us. It helped me become who I am today.

What stoked your imagination as a kid? Science fiction. I loved *Doctor Who*, and always thought it would be cool to have a robotic dog. Being on video chat reminds me of the teleportation in *Star Trek.*

Why did you become an astronaut? When my brother came home from college, he looked at my report card and said, "You're doing well in math and science. You can become an astronaut or an aerospace engineer." That stuck with me, but I chose to do things that made me happy in my career. I worked at Ford Motor Company as an engineer, but then the CIA called. You don't know what you're going to do for them (laughs), but it's exciting. At some point, I figured I was getting too old, so I applied to the Astronaut Corps. I had good experience as both a lab geek and an operator, so I felt qualified.

Do you currently lead a team of people? No, but as an astronaut, you're also a role model. I've had students come to me five years after giving them advice, and they tell me they're working in aero-

space. I'm almost in tears. As role models, astronauts lead, but from a different vantage point.

What's the toughest part of being a role model?
When I put on that astronaut uniform, I'm a blue beacon. Imagine if I yelled at a guy on the road if he cut me off while wearing the suit? I can't do that. Little kids want to give you the biggest hug ever. It's the cutest thing, but it's also a reminder: As an astronaut, I'm a public figure with responsibility.

I've heard spacewalk training is incredibly hard. Tell me about it? We learn how to operate a robotic arm. Physically, it's tricky to operate. But it's also mentally draining: You're concerned about impressing other people. Once you stop worrying, it's doable. There's a great expression in Russian, *praktika - mat' ucheniya*, which translates to "practice is the mother of learning." I tell students all the time that anything you don't know is hard.

Are you excited to go to space? It's been a long road. The journey is the creative part, and there's so much to learn along the way. Because once you achieve that thing, then what's next?

TAKEAWAYS

1 Projects won't go as planned. It's normal to be annoyed at first, but then you need to adapt and move forward to thrive.

2 Tough situations in your life are crucible moments—ones that define your character. How will you react?

3 You're likely a role model to someone at work. Team members will be inspired by your actions in challenging situations.

06/Race through Distractions.

Stay on course like this race car driver.

 PUSH NOTIFICATIONS. EMAILS. Meeting invites. These distractions are roadblocks in your focus. As a young creative, you'll feel compelled to respond right away. How do you get *anything* done?

Take inspiration from race car driver Hurley Haywood's experience in the 1975 Rolex 24, a grueling endurance race where mental resilience is key. The thick fog of the night is clouding the focus of the drivers. Haywood gets a call. "Should we cancel the race?" asks his crew chief.

"Set your watch, and time my next lap," Haywood responds, in a moment of resilience.

He ignores the fog and hammers through. "I saw this as an opportunity for our team to make up extra time. If you're not able to adapt to changing conditions, then you're not going to win," he says.

Haywood's team secures first place. By taking a calculated risk, he proves it's possible to cut through the distraction.

You can apply this same mindset to your work. Need to get into your creative zone? Turn off push notifications, and set your status to "Heads down," or another indication that you're focused. This will reduce the amount of time lost when you're switching context from task to task. Your boss will appreciate the final results.

A FEW USEFUL DIVERSIONS

THE COFFEE MAKER
Illustrator Marion Deuchars prefers a percolator. "Complex rituals offer greater distractions," she says, and that allows her extra time to think. "There's no way I can come into my studio and just start working."

A MESSY STUDIO
Twenty-one other artists used to share a studio with Deuchars, but now she's on her own. "If you don't have people around, you find something else." By tidying up the studio, she can mentally switch gears between tasks.

A HANDS-ON ART PROJECT
The act of painting stones provides Deuchars with a moment of active relaxation. "There was a point that I had to put them away, because it was so joyful and would distract me for hours," she says.

THE DOG
Deuchars will take her dog, Pip, for a walk. "He's a hound, so he's always on the hunt for any little furry thing." That forces her to be more observant of her surroundings and keeps her focused.

No. 07

THE

Pitch

DOESN'T NEED TO BE

P E R F E C T .

Boost a
bland meeting
with a paper
fortune teller.

LIKE THE HEADLESS HORSEMAN, you stampede into yet *another* meeting, but without a fully-formed idea in your noggin. Hey, it's not your fault—there are so many meetings, and you haven't had time to think about this one. But what if I told you that blank canvas in your head is an opportunity? Let's listen in on a meeting at *O, The Oprah Magazine*.

Late in the day, the art department is huddled around a conference table, brainstorming a perplexing story on the power of chance. The working title is "Moments of Grace." Art Director Angela Riechers is uninspired but needs to participate.

Team members are tossing out cliché ideas like four-leaf clovers and dice. Someone suggests hiring an illustrator who works with paper, which sparks a related idea for Riechers. She makes a paper fortune teller and tosses it on the table. "I was so bored, making something with my hands actually helped me," she admits. The following idea was to illustrate Mexican *Lotería* cards. "The cards have an element of chance and luck to them," says Riechers. "Plus, they're visually appealing." The team continues to build on this idea, exploring fortune cookies and other visual ephemera. Eventually they hire illustrator Eduardo Recife to create the finished product.

Riechers's experience demonstrates the power of actively listening and infusing your own interests into brainstorming sessions. While none of the individual pitches were perfect, they built on one another to eventually form a great idea.

Similar to Riechers, you won't be enthused about every meeting. Take notes, listen, and strike when the time is right.

 MY GROWTH PLAN

"Illustration is like climbing a mountain."

—

YUKO SHIMIZU'S FIRST CAREER OUT OF COLLEGE SUCKED. HERE'S HOW SHE ROSE TO THE TOP.

OCCUPATION
Illustrator, Adjunct Professor, School of Visual Arts

LOCATION
New York, New York

W

WHEN I WAS A TWO-YEAR-OLD in Japan, I took out a crayon, drew a line that went north, and added a circle to it. I said "Mom, I drew a balloon."

—

MY PARENTS WERE against the pursuit of art. The Japanese have a notion that creative occupations are very difficult. They want their kids to be doctors, lawyers, politicians, or businesspeople.

—

AS A CHILD, I could only recognize about ten people in my class. I have face blindness disorder.

—

I WENT TO A REGULAR university in Japan. My concentration was in advertising and marketing, because I thought it was the most creative thing to do in the practical, real world.

—

I TOOK A CORPORATE PR JOB, stayed in it for

ten years. It wasn't a glamorous job, nothing like Samantha Jones in *Sex in the City*.

—

WHEN I TURNED THIRTY, I asked myself, Is this really what I want to do? I knew how to draw but felt inferior to anyone that went to art school. The only way to overcome it was to move to New York and go to the School of Visual Arts. I saved up enough money from my PR job and moved to the United States.

—

MY FIRST ILLUSTRATION JOB was for the *Village Voice*. Black and white. Tom Cruise, Rosie O'Donnell, and David Hyde Pierce, coming out of the closet together.

—

TOM CRUISE WAS really hard to illustrate. I look at the work now, and it's total crap. But I was really proud to get paid $200 for it.

—

I TRY NOT TO TAKE ON projects that involve good-looking actors and actresses. Recently, I accidentally took on a job where I had to illustrate Brad Pitt. It was really hard. I printed his portrait really big and broke his facial features down into shapes. I really love graphic design, so I treated the challenge as pure composition.

—

COMING UP WITH NEW IDEAS is hard—you have to create something from scratch. Once I come up with the idea, I feel great, but then I have to sit in front of a piece of paper for hours and hours. But in a way, it's easier. I have something to compare it to. I never want to go back to my previous life in PR.

—

ILLUSTRATION IS LIKE climbing a mountain. I work hard. Sometimes the hill is easy; sometimes it's steep. When you reach the top, all is forgiven.

TAKEAWAYS

1

It's never too late to switch careers.

2

Reading can spark ideas for projects. Books flex your imagination. Set aside a time to read every day, even if just for ten minutes.

3

Travel adds to your personal experience, which enhances your imagination.

AFTER I GRADUATED from the School of Visual Arts, I had a year to find a work visa. After that, the visa would've expired and I wouldn't be allowed to work.

—

I WAS OFFERED TO TEACH a precollege class for high schoolers. They were in desperate need of a teacher of color. Later on, they gave me an undergraduate college class, and my immigration lawyer told me to never let that teaching job go. I needed it to keep my visa.

—

TEACHING KEEPS ME YOUNG. Right now, the kids are really into the 1980s, which is funny to me—they are dressing and liking things that I did when I was exactly their age. I tell them to look up artists from that time. We exchange information—they can learn something from me; I can learn something from them. Once you stop learning, you become old and grumpy.

—

I DON'T WATCH A LOT of movies, and I don't read graphic novels. I like traditional books with words. Books with words aren't visual, but that strengthens your imagination. It creates a better library in my brain, and that creates a better outcome in my work.

—

I TRAVEL A LOT. Mostly to conferences or workshops. I don't decide where I go. I meet people and experience local life wherever I go. Going to unplanned locations is an ideal way to be inspired and decompress. I don't use an iPad, so I can't bring my work with me. I read.

—

READING BOOKS about countries or places I have never been to—it forces me to imagine what the place looks like. Books are travel for the mind, and you don't have to spend any money.

▼
Zakiya Pope, on Writing Emails
"Strong subject line—I want you to open it. A quick greeting, short scannable bullet points, and then wrap that shit up."

One (and a Half) Things at a Time.

How to focus when your to-do list is raining down like an asteroid shower.

YOUR MISSION: REMAIN creative and productive on a daily basis. *But how will you get it all done?* Just ask astronaut Jeanette Epps.

Epps is underwater in NASA's Neutral Buoyancy Lab, training for the spacewalk, which she says is "one of the hardest things an astronaut has to do." Clock is ticking. Six hours to complete a barrage of tasks, such as tightening bolts, changing batteries, and screwing in light bulbs. Epps is sporting a bulky pressurized suit, which multiplies the difficulty of subaquatic movement and replicates the feeling of being in space.

Epps steels her mind. "Remain present, and think, *This is the most important thing I'm doing right now,*" she says.

Here's how you can apply Epps's wisdom to your work. Choose a key creative task, such as designing comps for your director. This is your "full-task," one that requires more creative energy. Next, pick a tactical task, such as file organization or emails. That's your "half-task," and it doesn't demand as much creativity.

Focus on your full-task until you hit a creative block. Close the file. Take a break, and move on to the half-task. Emails usually aren't fun, but they aren't terrible when they provide a break from challenging creative work. This process reframes the two tasks as rewards for one another, and charges you with renewed energy for the full-task.

Find the right balance of creative and tactical tasks in your day, and you too can achieve neutral buoyancy—the equal tendency of an object to sink or float. Sounds way better than career burnout.

Don't Try So Hard.

No.
09

INTRACTABLE PROBLEM? TAKE A BREAK AND LET YOUR SUBCONSCIOUS RUN THE SHOW.

ACCORDING TO ILLUSTRATOR MARION DEUCHARS, "THE RIGHT BRAIN INTERVIEWS THE LEFT BRAIN.

MR. SENSIBLE AND MR. CREATIVE HAVE A BATTLE," AND THE SOLUTION MAGICALLY APPEARS.

▼

**Leo Rodgers,
on His Power Suit**
*"Oddly enough, when I lost
my leg, my bike became my
prosthetic, because I don't
wear a prosthetic leg. My bike
makes me feel like Iron Man."*

Unleash Your Creative Power Suit.

A simple article of clothing is the cheat code for confidence.

I'M ABOUT TO GIVE MY FIRST BIG PRESENTATION FOR ADOBE. Can this black T-shirt boost my confidence? Because right now, I don't feel like I belong here **(1)**. When you're not feeling confident about the day ahead, regardless of whether or not you need to give a presentation, put yourself in a positive headspace with a creative uniform. By wearing an outfit you love, you project an image of who you *want to be*: a tool known as positive visualization **(2)**. The artist Georgia O'Keeffe was on Team Black Uniform, and she chose the color for its practicality—one less decision to fuss over in the morning, therefore more time to paint in the day. ❡ When I was a young designer, I poured over design annuals, and the photos of the black-clad creative directors always stirred wonder. Today, wearing all black **(3)** makes me *feel* like a creative director, and that scuttles any unwanted insecurities. ❡ Okay, it's presentation day. Before I utter the first few words of *x-Heighted* **(4)**, I feel like a combination of all my design heroes. I deliver my talk without a single stutter on stage **(5)**. And thankfully, the black T-shirt hid my pit stains **(6)**. Blazer, boots, or band T-shirt, your favorite outfit will turn up your confidence when you're feeling down.

① Reminisce on your successes that led to this big moment. It'll remind you that you deserve this.

② Practice mindfulness in the morning. Imagine yourself succeeding at the end of the day.

③ A unique article of clothing is a great icebreaker. I wear a lapel pin instead of a pocket square.

④ Take deep belly breaths right before a stressful event. It'll relax your nervous system.

⑤ Keep a journal of big victories. You can draw upon those memories in stressful situations.

⑥ Forgot to say something? Don't backpedal. You're the only person who knows.

THE ULTRA-MARATHONER

Q

+

A

DISCOVER **DEAN KARNAZES**'S SECRETS FOR WRITING FIVE BOOKS AND RUNNING HUNDREDS OF MILES, OCCASIONALLY AT THE SAME TIME.

LOCATION
Kentfield,
California

▼

ULTRAMARATHONERS MAY SEEM LIKE superhumans, achieving feats that feel out of reach for most of us. Karnazes's list of accomplishments includes: a run in the frigid South Pole, a run in the torrid Death Valley, and a run that spanned three days...without sleep. In speaking with Karnazes, my goal was not to marvel at his physical accolades, but to examine his mental drive. For someone nicknamed The Ultramarathon Man, he's a humble guy, with insatiable curiosity and a tremendous work ethic. Here's how he gets it all done.

Why do you write? (Laughs) Wow. You came out of the gate with a tough one. Kidding aside, I write because it's hard. I write because I want to live up to my potential. I don't think I'll ever master the craft of writing—no piece of writing is ever perfect.

What's your key to endurance? Variety. There's a lot of creativity in what I pursue as a runner. Some runners like to run marathons; others run around the neighborhood. I pride myself on being a prolific runner versus a fast runner. I like to do everything from short 5Ks to 200-mile (322-km) ultramarathons. I like to make up adventures. Next weekend, I'm going to Greece with a friend. We're going to watch the sunrise from the Acropolis and then run 48 miles (77 km) to Athens to watch the sunset. It's not a race, just what I think is a good idea and a fun thing to do.

Do you write while you run? All the time. I used to carry a digital recorder. Now, I just dictate writing into my phone. As a runner and a writer, you can probably attest—we have some of our clearest thoughts while out running.

What do you think about while running? The big answer is that I think about a lot of things, and I think about nothing. Running gives you the freedom to not be bombarded by noise. My mother was an English teacher, and she used to say, "The best writers are the best readers." Training as much as I do, I don't have as much time to sit and read physical books as I'd like. I have five hundred audiobooks on my playlist, so I listen while I run.

I'm listening to Dave Grohl's audiobook. Did he read it himself?

Yes. It adds an extra layer, because his voice is so entertaining. The reader makes a big difference with audiobooks. I'm 100 percent Greek, and the first piece of literature, *Iliad* and *Odyssey*, was passed down orally. They were lyrical writers.

How does your Greek ancestry inspire your writing? I go to Greece, probably four or five times a year. I love reading the classics: Heraclitus, Aeschylus, and Homer. Reading a lot of Greek literature has really been instructive to my writing.

So much conflict in their work. What's your biggest conflict right now? I'm trying to figure out what really brings me fulfillment in life. Running is an element, but not the only one. I've written a screenplay inspired by Greek literature, and it's in the process of being produced by Hollywood. It was a challenge learning how to write in a different format than a novel or an autobiography.

What inspired you to write a screenplay? The combination of my love of classics and ancient Greece. During the lockdown, I delved deep into ancient Athens. Greece is the birthplace of democracy, and that was not only interesting to me but relevant to current times. Socrates was a really quirky, compelling person, and I just thought, What if I make him into a movie character?

Whom do you collaborate with? My wife. She's brutal. When you write, you want honest feedback—someone to say that a phrase is cliché. My wife will cross out entire paragraphs. I've never written a screenplay, so I need her help.

Sounds like new challenges inspire you. When it comes to both running and writing, I'm allergic to routine. I'm not one of those authors that can get up every morning at five o'clock and pump out one thousand words for my book. If the process feels mundane, then it feels like work.

Writing and running are kinda the same, huh? Yes. They're both inherent in us: 1 percent inspiration, 99 percent perspiration.

TAKEAWAYS

1 Variety is the key to endurance. Shake up the routine of your creative process by changing the time or place you work.

2 Running inspires writing because it allows your subconscious mind to process the creative work.

3 Every writer needs an editor, and every creative needs a second opinion. Find someone who's honest.

11/Rest for Greater Success.

Take a break and pick up a side activity. It'll sharpen your mind.

"HARD WORK DULLS YOU AND recovery sharpens the knife," says Olympic Gold medalist Billy Demong.

In his sport of Nordic combined skiing, Demong needed to rest in order to keep his arms and legs sharp as blades. The athlete discovered that more than seven hundred hours of training was too far. "When you're trying to be the best, you need to be more recovered than ever before," he says.

As a creative, I may not plow down ski slopes at a breakneck speed of 60 mph, but my role is just as mentally taxing. The same principles of rest apply. After about two hours of writing, I feel foggy and need to recharge.

Sounds simple. But how do you take a break when your brain is on overdrive? Demong recovered physically while maintaining a sense of momentum by engaging his mind with side activities such as day trading, carpentry, and countertop building.

In my case, I'll step away from writing to draw a bird on my iPad. It focuses my mind on a creative task and distracts me from the writer's block. When I return, even if it's ten minutes later, I have an objective point of view and can immediately see areas for improvement in my writing.

Feeling blocked? Remember this: A well-rested mind is more powerful than a tired set of hands.

RELAX AND RECHARGE

PRACTICE YOGA
"Getting your body and mind centered is key," says Jeanette Epps. The astronaut practices yoga and cardio exercises to steel her mind for demanding tasks like operating the massive robotic arm at NASA.

PLAY THE GUITAR
Engaging in another creative task is a great way to let your subconscious kick in. David Cooper keeps nine guitars in his illustration studio and rips "Everlong" by the Foo Fighters when he's stumped.

WASH THE DISHES
"I think a lot without thinking," says professor Angela Riechers. She'll take a break to wash the dishes while planning the next class. "When I'm not churning in my mind, that's when the answer will pop up."

GO FOR A RUN
A midday run is essential when I'm working from home. I often feel groggy around 2 p.m., and a few miles on the treadmill will spark an unexpected idea for the design of *Fast Company*'s next cover.

▼

**Leo Rodgers,
on Riding Uphill**

*"I hate it, but I also love the
excitement of climbing. When I
get to see the view up top, I feel
like I've conquered something."*

End Your Day on Time.

This cyclist's fall can help you rise the next day.

LE BEATRICE. A LOVELY NAME FOR A treacherous course, littered with rocks that are just waiting to trip those who dare to traverse it. Mountain biker Evelyn Dong rides the mud-slathered trail, dialing in her technique before tomorrow's prestigious World Cup event.

Roaring spectators and members of the press add to the pressure. Dong hits a slippery stone barrage, slams the breaks too soon, and tumbles down the course. Crash. Fourth time today. "If you're full of fear, you lock up," she says. "There's no sense beating your head against a wall." Dong calls it a day.

Your version of the roaring crowds: clients and

SIMPLIFY THE FEEDBACK LOOP

**DON'T REVISE
SO QUICKLY**
You'll set an expectation that you're always available for more adjustments. If you can, let the client know that you'd like a "little time to think about it," and estimate when you'll take care of the revision. It's a thoughtful response that demonstrates how it takes time to make good work.

peers who need everything done. Right. Now. You're grinding. It's late. How do you know when to call it quits? Illustrator Yuko Shimizu takes a prudent approach: "Unless it's due that night, wait until tomorrow. Three hours at night equals one hour in the morning when you're fresh." When you're tired, your pace decreases and your frustration increases.

Celebrate your daily achievements like illustrator Marion Deuchars. The completion of a twenty-minute Spanish class and grocery shopping are two small wins that fill her day with positivity. But she's also realistic about what can be accomplished. "No one suffers if you don't send that email or miss the book deadline," she says. End your day on a high note.

The next day, Dong hops back on her bike, poised to charge through the competition with a clear head. Like our earlier example of race car driver Hurley Haywood, Dong tunes out the static of her surroundings. "When I think back, the spectators were a blur, and the trail ahead was clear." She finishes the race in twenty-seventh place. "That's not a big deal for anyone else except me," she says. The crash built Dong's resilience—she was able to reframe it into her own personal victory.

Set realistic goals. Close your day with a victory. Whether it's a genius idea or a pleasant conversation, you'll pocket a boost of energy for tomorrow.

No.

12

No.

Don't Always End Your Day on Time.

Especially if
Michael Jackson
is involved.

**STAY UP ALL NIGHT LIKE
DEAN KARNAZES**

I FINALLY GOT HOME FROM WORK AT 6 A.M. As the "late person" at *Entertainment Weekly,* I was responsible for approving every single page of the magazine before it went to press. To make matters worse, Michael Jackson had recently passed away.

While unfortunate, this experience is imprinted in my brain as one of my favorite nights of work.

Yes, working after-hours sucks. You should end your day on time. Most of the time. Unless you're creating something meaningful that can't wait until tomorrow.

At a time when print media was still a major news source, *Entertainment Weekly* couldn't wait until the next issue to cover the passing of a pop culture icon like Michael Jackson. And so, the staff went to work on a new issue. From scratch. We designed, wrote, and sourced photos at Olympic-level speed. With barely any time to think, designers relied on one another for quick feedback, making swift creative decisions, together. We charged into each other's offices with multiple versions of a single layout, huddling on the best direction to move forward with. It was hectic. It was intense. I loved it. My creative copilots alleviated the stress of making lightning-fast decisions, and I continually strive for this level of collaboration in my work today.

When the work is meaningful, an all-nighter will feel like a light jog. You'll see what you're *really* capable of, and that'll fuel your optimism for future challenges.

⊕	**CUT BACK ON CAFFEINE**	"Cut back significantly on caffeine the month before the all-night run. It'll be more potent that way," says Karnazes. Swap in warm water. Lemon. Ginger.
⊕	**TURN UP THE LIGHTS**	"Get a bright headlamp. The more lumens, the more your circadian rhythms will cease to kick into sleep mode," he says. No headlamp? Turn up the office lights.
⊕	**CLEAN UP YOUR DIET**	"Avoid too much sugar. Ditto on nuts, turkey, oats, and cheese. All are high in sleep-inducing tryptophan," he says. Peanut butter on celery makes for a filling snack.

▼
Marion Deuchars, on Deadlines
"There's always more to do. I'll always have an email or a sketch that I didn't get to. But no one dies if you miss a deadline, do they?"

SPRINT

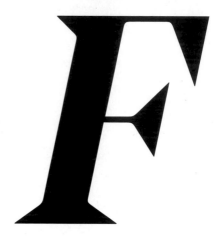

AS I LEAN INTO A LEFT TURN on my motorcycle, I'm ejected into the air. What the hell did I do wrong?

Moments before this, I felt my mind racing. *How do I work a manual shift? Is all this leather gear really necessary? Does Eve (my then-girlfriend) think I look cool on this bike?* And to make matters worse, this is my first time on a motorcycle.

How do you make quick creative decisions? The key: Don't overthink them.

After my own perplexing left me pancaked on the ground next to my bike, my instructor Tony Trauma rushes toward me. I laugh to myself: *Oh yeah, he warned me about this.* That morning, Tony told us over and over: "Do not slow down into a turn." He invoked the legendary pilot Chuck Yeager as a way to instruct us on how to handle speed. "When you take the bike around a turn, be just like Chuck," he'd say. "Go faster." The science makes sense: Speed maintains friction with the road, and the bike needs extra friction as it's unstable while turning.

I discovered the secret to design sprints while I was a budding associate art

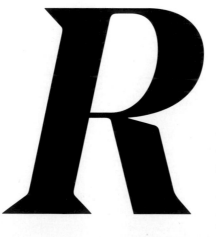

BY THINKING LESS.

The one tactic that enables you to rush in an hour.

director at *Entertainment Weekly*. Had to work quickly, no choice. Here's the deal: Design is a series of decisions. *Where does this shape go? What color should it be?* When I confidently make those decisions, the work looks sharp. But if I overthink it and worry what others think, the work suffers—self-doubt interrupts the logical sequence of creative decisions.

The next day, I return to the motorcycle class with fresh perspective. *Who cares what people think?* But then, Tony whispers in my ear, "You better pass. Eve just wants to ride on the back of the bike with you." The words bounce off my newfound body armor, and with Chuck Yeager-like precision, I weave in and out of the orange cones. Pass. Class M motorcycle license.

A year later, Eve and I got married. Easiest decision I ever made. Don't overthink your decisions. Trust your gut.

Following your intuition is clutch to enduring any project, short- or long-term. But it's only one tool for endurance. In the next section, you'll learn how Karin Fong uses research to jump-start the design of her title sequences.

No. 14

 MY GROWTH PLAN

"We still have a childlike excitement."

—

JAY OSGERBY EXPLAINS WHAT IT'S LIKE TO DESIGN AN OFFICE CHAIR FOR THE BIGGEST TECH COMPANY IN THE WORLD.

▪ **OCCUPATION**
Partner,
Barber Osgerby

▪ **LOCATION**
London,
England

MY JOB IS TO IMPROVE OBJECTS to accommodate a societal need. I'm responsible for putting stuff in the world. At the moment, that's a pretty heavy job—we don't need more things.

—

I WAS WORKING the lunch shift as a waiter in a restaurant in South Kensington. I got chatting to a couple of customers that were in the wine business. They were looking for someone to design a restaurant, so I gave an elevator pitch at the table. "If you need any help, I'm studying architecture up the road at the Royal College. I'd really like to help work on the project."

—

"YEAH, OKAY," THEY SAID. *I don't have a clue what I'm doing,* I thought.

—

I RIPPED OFF MY APRON after my shift and

ran back to college. I told Ed (his future partner at Barber Osgerby) about the project. On my own, I couldn't have done this. But with a partner, I had the confidence to pull it off.

—

ED AND I HAVE A LOVELY, fraternal relationship. He's one of three boys. I'm one of three boys. We still have a childlike excitement about design.

—

WHEN HE AND I DESIGNED the Tipton chair, we did a lot of research into how kids concentrate. When they push back in their chairs, they're not being naughty. Kids need to circulate blood, and they fidget in order to think.

—

ROLF FEHLBAUM, the CEO of Vitra, Mr. Vitra himself, called us up because he liked the Tipton chair. "We'd be interested in your take on the office chair of the future," he said to us.

—

ED AND I HIGH-FIVED each other all the way back to the airport. We were like, *We can't believe we just had that brief.*

—

UNTIL THAT POINT, office chairs expressed a machinelike quality. As an employee, when you sit on this machinelike object, you become a machine. Conceptually, we didn't like that.

—

OUR DESIGN WAS a direct response to the Aeron chair. They made the modern office feel like a Ridley Scott film. When you switch the lights off at night, the chairs feel like they are plotting to overthrow humanity.

—

IF YOU'RE A MUSICIAN, and you're working on your first record, you need to experiment a lot.

—

WE DESIGNED thirty different chairs.

TAKEAWAYS

1
Partnering with others offers a boost in confidence.

2
Don't worry if you don't have the necessary skills for an exciting project. Jump right in, and figure out how to do it later on.

3
Be mindful of the social impact of your work.

THE HARDEST PART was settling on a design.

—

AS WE WERE WORKING on it, Apple became interested in buying all of these chairs for their office. Foster + Partners, who was designing Apple Park, liked the architectural simplicity of our Pacific chair.

—

THE APPLE COMMISSION created a deadline, which helped us focus. We had a delivery date, and an order of about twelve thousand Pacific chairs.

—

THE PACIFIC CHAIR was designed to feel calm. Once we made that decision, the design process became very pragmatic. With modeling clay, we'd refine each part, like the forward tilt button or height adjustment lever, until it felt calm.

—

OUR SUBSEQUENT PROJECT was Soft Work, designed for Vitra. During the pandemic, there was a massive expansion in the freelancer economy. Workers needed to get away from the piles of laundry and their cats. They would go into a public space just to feel like they had colleagues.

—

SOFT WORK IS A CHAIR designed for people to work in public spaces. It's a chair-height, electrified sofa system, which actually became the ultimate office chair. You could have it in a hotel lobby or an airport. Funny enough, that actually became the office chair of the future.

—

I WANT TO DESIGN another chair now. If I were a musician, it would be like my third album. That's when the artist is really getting into their groove. I'd want the chair to feel totally different.

—

MY NEXT CHAIR WILL be my version of Radiohead's *OK Computer.*

TAKEAWAYS

TODAY'S
LEARNINGS
FOR A
BETTER
TOMORROW.

→ Just start moving. The idea will strike.

→ Need to focus? Turn off notifications and sprint. → The messages can wait. → Stumped? Pause on the creative task, handle the boring one. → Your subconscious will do the heavy lifting.

→ Speaking of what's going on upstairs: Your shirt communicates your mindset to the outside world. Give your outfit some thought. → Clear your head: Write down random ideas, and make room for fresh ones. → Bored in a meeting? Listen actively, and speak when the idea hits (bring that notebook). → Frustrated? Call it a day. It'll probably take you a third of the time tomorrow.

ACTIVITIES

SHARPEN YOUR PENCIL AND EXAMINE YOUR DAY.

▸ UNLEASH YOUR CREATIVE POWER SUIT.

P. 35

Think about a creative superhero who you'd like to embody. Draw them!

What are three qualities that you admire about them?

- [ ] ....
- [ ] ....
- [ ] ....

What article of clothing do you have to emulate them?

....

▸ DON'T ALWAYS END YOUR DAY ON TIME.

P. 41

Reflect on an all-nighter project. How'd you grow from the experience? Draw it.

You before

You after

▸ BREAK A BORING ROUTINE.

P. 25

Write your current routine, and think about when you're most creative. How can you rearrange your day to be more productive?

BEFORE

● Morning   ● Afternoon   ● Evening

AFTER

● Morning   ● Afternoon   ● Evening

► ONE (AND A HALF) THINGS AT A TIME.

P. 34

Let's prioritize. Focus on whatever task is high priority, and make a low-priority task your half task. The others can wait.

Task you need to complete
○ ○ ○ ○
Priority (1=Low 4=High)

Task you need to complete
○ ○ ○ ○
Priority (1=Low 4=High)

Task you need to complete
○ ○ ○ ○
Priority (1=Low 4=High)

Task you need to complete
○ ○ ○ ○
Priority (1=Low 4=High)

► REST FOR GREATER SUCCESS.

P. 39

List four short activities you can use as breaks from a project you're currently working on. Draw or write them!

1

2

3

4

► TEDIOUS TASKS? HIGHER PURPOSE.

P. 24

Distinguish the difference between tedious tasks that are meaningful and meaningless. What can you delegate?

Meaningful

☐ ....
☐ ....
☐ ....

Meaningless

☐ ....
☐ ....
☐ ....

Which can you delegate?

....

Your Project

SHARPEN YOUR CREATIVE PROCESS WITH THESE PRACTICAL STRATEGIES AND TOOLS.

▼ YOUR DAY

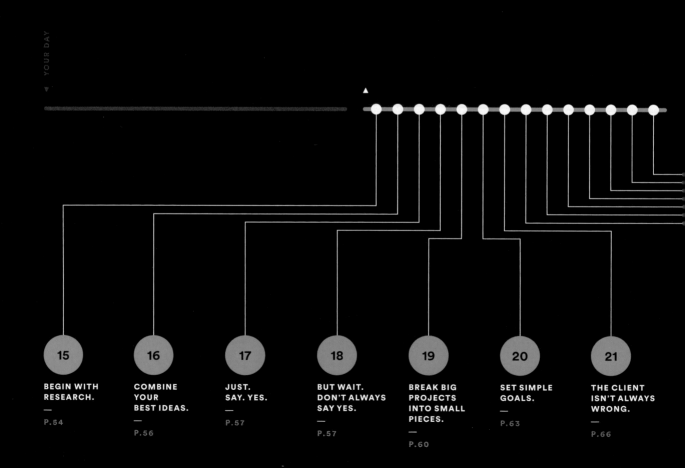

15

BEGIN WITH
RESEARCH.
—
P.54

16

COMBINE
YOUR
BEST IDEAS.
—
P.56

17

JUST.
SAY. YES.
—
P.57

18

BUT WAIT.
DON'T ALWAYS
SAY YES.
—
P.57

19

BREAK BIG
PROJECTS
INTO SMALL
PIECES.
—
P.60

20

SET SIMPLE
GOALS.
—
P.63

21

THE CLIENT
ISN'T ALWAYS
WRONG.
—
P.66

"You never want to present two ideas that are

similar—they take away from each other."

—SAGI HAVIV

▼

P.59

▼
Yuko Shimizu, on That Light Bulb Moment
"I need to do research for every job. Knowing more helps me create better images. I rarely have that light bulb moment without research."

15 / Begin with Research.

Spark creative ideas by literally lighting things on fire.

 A BURNING FORTUNE COOKIE tumbles across the screen. Curtains engulf in flames. A high school varsity jacket melts. This is the title sequence for *Little Fires Everywhere*, and the design firm Imaginary Forces scorched all of the props on set.

The title sequence for a TV show is one of the most labored pieces of design. But how do you get your audience to resist that "Skip Intro" button?

Create a clever concept that makes the viewer feel an emotion. Step one: research. That will lead you to a metaphor, one of Creative Director Karin Fong's favorite conceptual tools. For a solid example, let's dig deeper into *Little Fires Everywhere*.

While combing through the books and the script, Fong's team unearthed a series of objects, like shoes and a violin, which had greater emotional meaning for the characters on the show. Boom! The metaphor. On the last day of filming, when the props were no longer needed, they were set on fire. Real, live, incinerating, superhot, "you need a pyrotechnic on set," "you only have one chance, so don't mess it up" fire.

Stoked to start a project? Hit pause for a moment. Let's reflect: Had Fong skipped the critical stage of research, those flammable metaphors may have eluded her, and the final product wouldn't be so explosive. Do your research. Worth it.

IGNITE YOUR IMAGINATION

(+) CLEAR YOUR HEAD
You have a personal style, but try to avoid going into a project with an answer. The end result will feel surprising for you and collaborative for the client.

(+) CONDUCT INTERVIEWS
Conversation allows you to focus on interesting points and ask questions in real time. Research your subject ahead of time so you can ask more specific questions.

(+) CREATE A STRUCTURE
While researching, you'll uncover more information than necessary. Focus by writing a problem statement. This will help you identify useful information.

(+) BE FLEXIBLE
Structure is important, but don't be rigid. Creativity is iterative. Experiment with a variety of approaches in the beginning. The end result may change dramatically.

No. **16**

Combine Your Best Ideas.

What do a baseball,
a grenade, and a row of planes
have in common?

1

DIVERGENCE

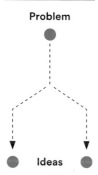

Problem

Ideas

Write a problem statement, and ask your team to prototype a variety of ideas. This process can apply to other creative fields, such as writing or painting.

LEADING A BIG PROJECT AND STRUGGLING TO UNIFY YOUR team's ideas? Take a cue from the elaborate title sequence for Jack Ryan. Creative director Karin Fong used a process called divergence **(1)** and convergence **(2)** to achieve, as she says, "continual aha moments for the viewer." During the divergence phase, team members independently generate a variety of ideas, and during convergence, the best ideas are selected and formed into a coherent whole. This collaborative process was integral to the complexity of the title sequence. ❡ The show opens with an ominous overhead shot of men rowing a boat, juxtaposed against a whizzing bullet. Glitching visual combinations continue to roll: a plane propeller and a ceiling fan, a grenade with a baseball, a row of planes and a spinal column. During the divergence phase, designers made two discoveries: the side-by-side juxtapositions while exploring a direction called "duality," and the glitching effect, which surfaced from a direction called "pattern recognition." These ideas converged into a final sequence that appears "as if a supercomputer generated a portrait of Jack Ryan," according to Fong. "Riffing off each other is one of the most fun parts."

2

CONVERGENCE

Ideas

Solution

You may not arrive at the final solution after the first round of divergence and convergence. Identify what works, and repeat the process until you get there.

No.

17

Just.
Say.
Yes.

How a flight to
Texas can lead
to a series of
dream projects.

THE PHONE RINGS. "YOU STILL live in Dallas, right?" a photo editor from *Rolling Stone* asks photographer Peter Yang. "Uh, yeah. I live there," he responds.

Yang does not live there.

Breaking into the creative industry means accepting projects that may not seem ideal. A tight budget, a quick turnaround, or, in Yang's case, a distant location can be discouraging. However, the right project could lead to bigger and better career-shaping opportunities.

Rolling Stone needs a photographer to shoot the up-and-coming band My Chemical Romance and assumes Yang still lives in his hometown in Texas. Thrilled for the opportunity, he hops on a plane to Dallas on his own dime—an optimistic move when you're in your twenties and blowing a lot of your cash on your NYC apartment. But he senses an opportunity. "I just got my ass there," Yang tells me as we discuss his career.

"I remember thinking, I really want to shoot for *The New York Times Magazine*," he adds. "Literally a week later, they called with a cover for Stephen Colbert." Yang continued to photograph celebrities ranging from Taylor Swift to Kevin Durant and even legendary author Kurt Vonnegut. Shelling out the cash for a flight to Texas paid off in dividends.

So how do you know when to say yes? If the project is exciting, the client seems especially collaborative, or you'll learn a new skill, go for it.

While not every low-paying, distant project will lead to the big break, the more chances you take, the greater your chances are of success.

But Wait. Don't Always Say Yes.

No.

IF THE TIMELINE IS TOO COMPRESSED, PROJECT REQUIREMENTS AREN'T CLEAR (AFTER ASKING FOR FURTHER CLARIFICATION), AND/OR THE PERSON APPROVING YOUR WORK IS OVERLY FRENZIED, DISORGANIZED, OR WRITES WITH A LOT OF TYPOS. RED FLAGS FOR A DISASTEROUS PROJECT.

 MY GROWTH PLAN

"Fight for the things you really want."

—

SAGI HAVIV HAS DESIGNED LOGOS FOR THE BIGGEST BRANDS IN THE WORLD. BUT SUCCESS DIDN'T COME SO EASY AT FIRST.

OCCUPATION
Partner, Chermayeff & Geismar & Haviv

LOCATION
New York, New York

GROWING UP ON A KIBBUTZ informed my idea of teamwork from the very beginning. The children all lived together in a house on a commune in Israel, and that means everyone has an equal say. There's no room for egos. At our design firm, all of the partners are equals.

—

I DREW A LOT OF plants as a child. My mom got permission for me to go to an art school outside of the kibbutz. I wasn't accepted the first time, but I applied again as a sophomore. I got in.

—

WHEN I DIDN'T get into Cooper Union, I was devastated. That school was the reason that I came to the United States. It's scholarship based, and I couldn't afford to go to any other college.

—

I WOULD RIDE my bike in the city, and I couldn't

go past the foundation building on Astor Place. I would take a detour to avoid it. It symbolized failure—this was my hill to conquer.

—

I NEEDED A VISA to stay here, so I went to school for method acting. This was a place where I grew on a human level. The method is about sensory memory—the actor is really experiencing what the character is going through.

—

I PLAYED THE main character from *Dangerous Liaisons*. I'd say a line onstage, and the teacher would say, "What the fuck are you doing?" It was such a shame to spoil such a great piece.

—

YOU NEED TO FIGURE out what you're really passionate about, and do it. I didn't want to do anything that I wasn't great at.

—

WHEN I FINALLY graduated from Cooper Union, I was enamored with Chermayeff & Geismar. They had such a consistent portfolio of simple logos. It was the only place I wanted to work. They liked my portfolio, but weren't hiring.

—

I SAID, "OKAY, I'll come work for free. Three days a week."

—

BY WORKING FOR FREE, I saw it as an opportunity to prove myself. When I got my first paycheck, that was a big day.

—

IVAN AND TOM taught me so much. It's one thing to be able to design a logo that's nice, simple, and memorable. It's even harder to convince a client to adopt it.

—

AT FIRST, we lost the bid to design the U.S. Open Tennis logo.

TAKEAWAYS

1
If you've faced rejection, dust yourself off, and try again. Worked twice for Haviv!

2
Teamwork makes the dream work, on the kibbutz and at the design firm.

3
Clients will always want the final sooner: quality > speed.

WE WERE VERY excited because we're huge tennis fans. We went up to White Plains, and presented our credentials as part of a bid for the project. We got a call from a woman named Nicole. "Sorry, guys. We decided to go with another agency." I replied, "Okay. Call us anytime."

—

TWO AND A HALF months later, Nicole called again. "You told me I can call you anytime. We tried another firm, and we want to have you do the logo," she told me. We agreed to complete the project in six weeks.

—

DAYS LATER, SHE called again and asked me if we could complete it in four weeks. I said, "No, we need the time." You need to protect your product.

—

FUNNY ENOUGH, the logo they picked was born four days before our presentation. We had another version that we created weeks ago. We loved it. But it was too similar to the new one that we really loved. You never want to present two ideas that are similar—they take away from each other.

—

IF WE HAD AGREED to present it in two weeks, they would never have had this logo. This taught me a lot about insisting on the timeline, even if it causes the client heart palpitations.

—

IT'S A REALLY SCARY thing to push back on a client's timeline. We can do that because we know what it takes to get to a successful outcome, and Ivan, Tom, and I are all aligned. When you work collaboratively with equals, you can first figure out internally the right approach and then act on it with confidence.

—

I'M STANDING ON the shoulders of two giants. Because of them, I can see further.

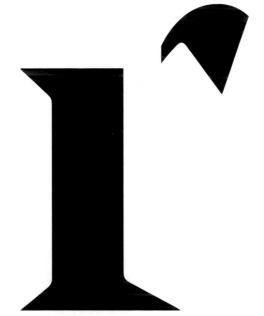

taking the next step to the best of my ability, and then the next step, and then the next step," he says. "It's a Zen-like experience and helps me get through anything."

This approach doesn't stop with runners. For example, creatives can break big projects into smaller achievable pieces. Designing a food delivery app is daunting but feels manageable when you focus on one screen at a time.

The design of a typeface is also a monumental task—one must create a visually cohesive family of twenty-six letters, ten digits, and punctuation, all in

WHO WOULD'VE EXPECTED that a traffic cone would prove to be a formidable foe for The Ultramarathon Man, aka Dean Karnazes?

During his nineteenth marathon in a series of fifty across the United States, Karnazes loops around this traffic cone during a tedious out-and-back race in Arizona. The sight of this devious orange plastic villain throttles his mind fast-forward. *Thirteen more miles to go? Thirty-one more races after this?*

Karnazes builds momentum by remaining hyperpresent. "I think about

 A SHORT STORY ABOUT CLIMBING A TALL MOUNTAIN

Extreme athlete Noah Galloway is struggling to hike up Mount Kilimanjaro. Running on fumes, Galloway has been awake since the middle of the night, with the goal of reaching base camp by sunset. Lack of sleep isn't an issue. Noah's years in the army have equipped him with the tool of false motivation to push through tough times. He explains, "Sometimes you have to convince yourself that you really want to achieve a goal, and you'll do whatever it takes to get there." But an insurmountable obstacle appears before Galloway:

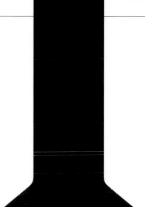

BIG PROJECTS INTO SMALL PIECES.

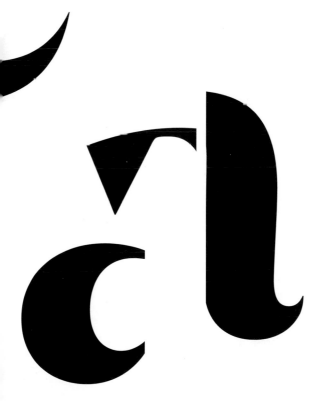

multiple weights. Type designer Rui Abreu utilizes a similar focus as Karnazes to get the job done. While it used to take Abreu four years to complete a font family, these days he's nailed down the sweet science and designed the typefaces Flecha and Rizoma in a single year.

His secret? Micro-focus. "I'll look at the brackets of the serifs or the diagonal strokes," says Abreu. "If another issue comes up, I'll make a note and fix it at another time." He gamifies the tedious work by chipping small items off his list, one by one. This technique can be applied to any field. Working on a long essay? Dedicate a day to rephrasing sentences or making your voice more active. You'll stay focused and feel productive.

Breaking a big project into small pieces is key to emotional satisfaction in any field. "The feeling of moving is fulfilling," says Abreu. "It's healthy to end a day with a sense of accomplishment."

One person runs fifty marathons in a row, and the other designs a typeface in a single year. Here's how.

altitude sickness. The higher he climbs, the more severe the symptoms become—a cruel reward for his valiant efforts. His

tour guide continues to tell him *polepole*, which is Swahili for "move slowly." Eventually, he passes out.

Initially feeling like a failure for not completing the hike, Galloway finds a silver lining. "I went seven rounds with that mountain and it

took it knocking me out to stop me." Big projects may break you down, but they also build your capacity for the next round.

20/Set Simple Goals.

An architect shares his keys for building a successful project plan.

 THE BUILDING STARTED WITH a pile of rubble. Steel beams crept toward the sky. Five thousand tiles of white marble covered those beams. Layers of glass were book-matched between the marble.

For every day of my walk to the *Fast Company* office, I was in awe of the gradual construction of the massive 90,000-foot (27,432-m)-tall Perelman Performing Arts Center. I continued to think: "What's it like to work on a project for this long?" So I reached out to Joshua Ramus, principal of REX, the architecture firm responsible for this building.

While the project took a decade, simple goals are Ramus's key to creative success. "Articulate why the goals are the embodiment of the needs of the user, and the debate about aesthetics goes away," says Ramus. In other words: art with purpose.

There were three goals for the Perelman PAC:

1. The stone facade had to be translucent.
2. The form of the building itself had to be simple.
3. The auditorium needed to be reconfigurable.

Align with your client on the goals for the user, and you'll keep the project in perspective. If a client asks for a change, and it doesn't affect one of your goals, then so be it. Keep your eyes on the prize. "You have the freedom to do what you want," says Ramus.

Oh, and the stone facade of the PAC glows at night.

A SMOOTH START TO YOUR PROJECT

CALL A KICKOFF MEETING
Gather everyone's ideas in the beginning, and they will be more invested in solutions that you present later on. Summarize these ideas in a shared document.

LEARN ABOUT THE CONSTRAINTS
They might be budget, time, resources, or just the aesthetic preference of someone in the meeting. Better to know about these sooner than later.

EMPHASIZE A PHRASE
Listen for keywords that you find inspiring. If someone says, "We want it to feel dynamic," reuse the word "dynamic" to form a bond.

SHARE VERSIONS
I like the rule of threes. Create a version that's conservative, one that's far out there, and one right in the middle. Options help a client feel involved.

THE MOUNTAIN BIKER

Q + A

EVELYN DONG LEAPS OFF MOUNT BOREDOM BY TRYING NEW TRICKS. TACTICS FOR TAKING YOUR STRETCH GOALS TO A NEW ELEVATION.

LOCATION
Salt Lake City, Utah

EVELYN DONG IS A FORCE TO BE reckoned with in the world of cross-country mountain biking, thanks to her boundless curiosity. "The unknown keeps me motivated," she says. "If you've ridden a course a million times, you already know you can do it." When she's not breezing past competitors on 100-mile (161-km) courses, she's lending her creativity to her other job in the bike shop, where she finds her moment of Zen while lacing up spokes on bike tires. "Patience is one of my strong points," she says.

What excites you about mountain biking? It's evolved over the years. I just got really into jumping. It's a whole new challenge.

Tell me about a great jump. There's a trail called bobsled in Salt Lake City. You jump over vintage cars, about 15 feet (4 m) in the air. Those are good learning jumps and the perfect level of adrenaline for me right now. There's a fear factor: If you make a mistake, then you crash-land on a pile of rusty metal.

What's so appealing about the danger of a jump to you? Once you get a little taste of what it's like to be in the air, it's addictive. You think about jumping all of the time, and that initial feeling of fear fades away. But if you overthink it, and you're scared going into the jump, then you will crash.

The idea of "not overthinking it" has come up in a lot of my interviews. I know athletes who analyze every single little thing, and that works for them. I like to move fast—it turns off the talky side of my brain and puts me in that flow state.

You tune out all the distractions. I need to be singularly focused on biking. Women are supposed to be good at multitasking. I'm not. Music and podcasts are great, but I can't listen while riding.

What if you can't get into your flow? Keep pushing, and hopefully you snap into that state. If it doesn't happen, you can't be too hard on yourself.

How is mountain biking creative? When you look at a trail, there are a million different lines. Even if it looks like a narrow single-track trail, just the way you approach it, and what you can see, it really varies from person to person. I was lucky to learn how from people who told me, "Don't be afraid to touch both sides of the tape."

What does that mean? The course is taped on both sides. If you're touching both sides of the tape, you're exploring the full parameters of the course. That's creative, because you're figuring out your own path.

How do you measure success? There are races where I've done really well. It's a very *blah* feeling. There are races where I've overcome personal battles or succeeded at riding a challenging feature. Those are more fulfilling.

Are you competitive? I've gotten less competitive over the years. I don't have to be the fastest every single day. Sometimes, it's best to just go out on the course and have fun.

What are you excited to do next in your career? I love coaching kids. They start out scared, but then ride the mountain bike and realize it's not that bad. I love the moment when it clicks. Kids can be more fun to coach than adults. Adults are more self-conscious and afraid, and that makes it really hard for them to learn new things.

How do you help adults learn? I share the same goofy tips that I tell kids. That breaks the ice and loosens them up to learn.

Do you consider yourself an optimist? "It'll go" is my catchphrase. It's a bit of a running joke. It means the feature that we're testing is doable. If I'm riding on a new course or testing out new features, like a jump, I'm generally the one that's like, "Yeah, it'll go."

What about trying new courses keeps you motivated? If you've ridden a course a million times, you know exactly how to do it. If you get complacent in whatever you do, that's when things get boring. Constantly pushing yourself makes you better.

 TAKEAWAYS

1 Tackle new challenges to unlock creative growth. That could mean a new job or a new technique for a project.

2 Tune out distractions to hop into that magical flow state. Creative in the morning? Save the production work for the afternoon.

3 Success is subjective. Personal growth and achievements can be more fulfilling than trophies and awards.

No.

21

▼
Yuko Shimizu, on Talent and Hard Work
"There's so much talent out there. It isn't enough to rely on talent and not work hard. You need to be able to take client feedback."

The Client Isn't Always Wrong.

How to flip a negative into a positive.

"IT WAS EXCELLENT. BUT CAN WE TALK about it?" The type of email that creatives dread.

Huh? Tom Geismar and Sagi Haviv are confused. They literally just presented the new ClearMotion branding to founders Shak Avadhany and Zack Anderson and thought it went great. What happened?

Avadhany and Anderson loved one slide of the presentation, where the logo is a pin on a person's jacket. The ovals are outlined instead of solid. But that wasn't Haviv's original intention for the design.

Haviv was initially taken back by this email, as he'd spent a lot of time pondering the form of this logo. ClearMotion, used by companies like Audi and Tesla, is a piece of software that reduces vibrations in a car through the scientific concept of laminar fluidity. Haviv distilled this confounding idea into an elegant visual solution of two solid interconnected ovals of different sizes, with negative space where they overlap.

They're telling us what the best version is?! Haviv thinks.

But then, he realizes the client is right. "The original logo had problems in small sizes," says Haviv. "We changed it, and suddenly it works even better."

As creatives, it's easy for us to take personal offense to feedback—our projects are like our babies. But if the client's suggestion improves the project, then go for it. Because in the end, you just want it to be kickass and amazing. Right?

CLIENT COLLAB 101

Five steps to establishing a more productive creative partnership.

ESTABLISH A RELATIONSHIP

"When we work with a client, we develop a doctor and patient relationship," says Haviv. "You're job is to provide them with the best solution."

GIVE AND TAKE

Metaphor alert! You're not arm-wrestling your client, you're operating a two-person saw with them. When they push, you pull, and vice versa.

BE HONEST

If you don't like a suggestion, push back. "You're not just there to do what you're told," says Haviv. When the client sees a great final product, they'll be happy.

AVOID GROUPTHINK

If the client proposes solutions before you've had a chance to present, politely ask for time to work. Give them a timeframe of when you'll return with your solution.

SHOW THE GOOD AND BAD

If they are adamant about something they want, do it, but also create the version you really want. Seeing what *doesn't* work might help them see what *does* work.

The Client Isn't Always Right.

What's your backup plan when Ryan Gosling suggests a bad idea?

RYAN GOSLING REQUESTED A SECOND Ryan Gosling on the set of his *Esquire* cover shoot.

Ludicrous? Yes. But this was the agreed condition of the photo shoot. Gosling was granted permission to conceptualize the photography—a rarity for magazines, but *Esquire* was willing to bend the rules for one of Hollywood's biggest stars. "I hated this," says design director David Curcurito. "I'm used to including celebrities on their concepts, but this was different. I didn't want to be told what to do with our magazine."

As a senior-level creative who understands the difference between a good and bad idea, how do you stay creative when forced to work with a stinker?

No.

SURVIVE A SOUR PROJECT

FEEL IT OUT
It's okay to be ticked, but don't be consumed by it.

IT'S NOT YOU
One sideways assignment is not a reflection of your talent.

MOVE ON
"We always have a next issue" was my bosses' mantra at *Entertainment Weekly*. Our work would be on newsstands for only seven days.

Gosling's ideas were based on his dreams, and he'd often call Curcurito in the middle of the night to share them. A nightmare of a photo made its way into the magazine: Ryan Gosling sitting on the couch, with another Ryan Gosling sitting in the window, and a woman painted as a skeleton. Curcurito and the team at *Esquire* came to a realization—they could make a virtue out of this bizarre photo shoot. A great example of cognitive reappraisal.

The headline on the cover says it all. "Welcome to the Ryan Gosling Freak Show. This cover was his idea. Both of him." *Esquire* wrote the feature on how strange the experience was. "Rather than try to make something weird look normal, we just let it look weird," Curcurito tells me.

One of the oddest passages from the *Esquire* story: "His apartment is full of skeletons. I give them nervous systems made from Christmas lights."

Strange situations like these build your resilience. Try not to fixate on the worst-case scenario. "In difficult circumstances where something goes against what you normally do, go with the flow, and modify your original story," says Curcurito.

The world doesn't know all of the struggles of a project—they only know the end result. Stuck with a bad idea? Own it. Harness the calamity like a lightning rod, and cast the illusion that it was intentional.

 MY GROWTH PLAN

"You're never really done."

—

WHETHER HE'S ROWING A BOAT OR DESIGNING A BUILDING, THE ARCHITECT **JOSHUA RAMUS**'S PROCESS IS RELENTLESS.

OCCUPATION
Principal,
REX

LOCATION
New York,
New York

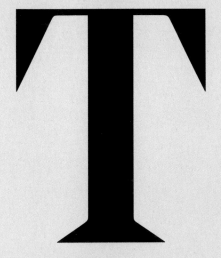

THE BEST ROWERS actually don't race anyone else. They look like they're out of it, because they're just simply in their own space. The moment they react to another rower, they lose their focus, overexert themselves, and blow up.

—

WHEN I WENT to graduate school at Harvard, I started training seriously for the '96 Olympics. I was ultimately knocked out in the semifinals, but I was still a very efficient athlete.

—

IN ROWING, you're attempting to perfect a single motion. Over and over. You might train the catch (the propulsive phase where the oar enters the water) for an entire day. In architecture, there is an iterative process where you continue to ask questions to find the perfect embodiment of an idea. Both rowing and architecture are relentless.

THE OLDER WE GET, the more we have to train ourselves to keep a child's mind.

—

AT OUR FIRM, we put a lot of trust in younger people who haven't become as battle weary as some of the senior members. They see things in ways that are unconventional.

—

WE REALLY LIVE with our projects, sometimes for over a decade. There are so many forces that could devolve a project. You just have to be the last person standing and not give up.

—

WHEN I WORKED on the Seattle Public Library, there was not a design decision on that building that wasn't the result of a rigorous analysis. That was the building that gave me my start.

—

LIBRARIANS ARE VERY educated but spend a lot of time showing people where books are. We wanted to make their jobs easier by making the book collections so incredibly obvious to navigate.

—

WE ARGUED THAT you could take the Dewey Decimal System and just make it a linear organization from 000 to 999. Our rule was that you'd never be allowed to disrupt it.

—

GIVEN THE NUMBER of books and the size of the site we had in Seattle, the only way to make that work would be to make the interior a continuous spiral.

—

THE ITERATIVE PROCESS continued to make things more interesting. Keep throwing challenges at a project, and it gets better. We asked, "Is this continuous spiral a problem for the disabled community?" As a result of that question, we built a rectangular spiral—like a parking garage.

(**TAKEAWAYS**)

1
Don't compare yourself with others. Run your own race.

2
Ask questions. Specific answers can lead to more interesting creative solutions.

3
Maintain a child's curiosity throughout your career. Fresh perspective!

SEATTLE SITS ON the worst fault line in North America. Conventional office buildings that are vertical are inefficiently designed for a catastrophic earthquake. The Seattle Public Library is a series of staggered boxes that are "pre-quaked." They're off center from each other and have a diagrid on the outside. It's designed to react to the force of an earthquake.

—

THE DESIGN OF THE building was so weird when we first unveiled it. It looks like everything was driven by an aesthetic desire, but there was no way anyone would have sketched it like that.

—

FROM ONE ANGLE, the building is ugly, but it's okay because it's so beautiful from other angles. That tension of one awkward moment is the result of relentless questioning.

—

THROUGH ROWING, I learned how to ride the razor's edge of exertion.

—

YOU NEED TO critically question yourself. When I make a form, I ask, "Did I make this for me? Is it in pursuit of the goal? Or is it adding cost and making me feel creative?"

—

I HAVE A TATTOO of a line by e.e. cummings: "Always the beautiful answer who asks a more beautiful question."

—

I LIVED NEXT to the World Trade Center in 2001. Like many people, it took a long time to digest. I can't understand it and will never understand it. I'm going to have to live with it as a question.

—

ARCHITECTURE IS AN iterative process, and you're never really done. You live with questions. The beauty is living with the question.

REVISE

"IS THAT ALL YOU'VE GOT?" my creative director asks me. Apparently, twenty revisions of this magazine feature aren't enough.

Revisions are often viewed as a reflection of our shortcomings as a creative. But, what if we use them as an opportunity to evolve our skills?

The creative director is meticulous, talented, and pushes me to the brink of my abilities. As a young designer, I want to earn my stripes and prove my worth. With printouts tucked under my arm,

I tap on their door. Flop sweating as I wait, thirty seconds feels like thirty hours when you're on deadline. I'm summoned to enter and nervously place my stack of layouts on their desk. One by one, my layouts are fired onto the floor, as if a high-speed conveyor belt is bolted onto the creative director's desktop.

"Guess I'll start over. Thanks!" I reply, unaffected. *Wait, who is this person?*

A crucible moment in my career. Energized by failure, my nervousness converts into resilience. I reframe this as one step toward my growth. *My next round of layouts will be even better.*

> Hold on loosely (to your project). If you cling too tightly, you're gonna lose control.

AREN'T THAAAAAT BAD.

My next round of layouts are thrown on the floor.

The creative director decides that we should work on the layout together, which means *they* will work on it, while I sit and watch. My layout is dismantled like a ticking time bomb, as if this were a scene in *The Hurt Locker*. Is the design better or worse? I can't tell, but after forty-five minutes, I'm ordered to finish the job.

The rinse-and-repeat process of that cycle occurs multiple times at this job, and I'm a better designer because of it.

I gleaned a few fragments of wisdom from the revision experience:

1. Design is subjective to opinion.

2. If someone doesn't love your work, find humor in the situation.

3. With grit, you can uncover infinite solutions to a problem. Exciting!

Another round of revisions? Let's face it: They're not as delightful as a daiquiri on vacation, but they aren't the apocalypse either. If you're peeved, take a cue from earlier in this book, and slow down your response. Reframe the revisions as an opportunity to grow, and they'll be a lot easier to swallow.

No. 23

▼
Leo Rodgers, on Falling
"When I spill off my bike, I stay optimistic. I think: I got my one fall out of the way for the day, and now I'm good to go."

PUT YOUR ERRORS ON TRIAL.

No.

24

Marie Kondo and the art of organizing your cluttered ideas.

MARIE KONDO IS poised in a curvy modernist chair, wearing a serene smile and a red blouse, waiting patiently for me to complete the design of her cover story for *Fast Company*. No, we're not together. In fact, I've never met her before. But I *feel* like I know her, as I've been staring at this photo of her for weeks.

The organizing consultant is the cover subject for *Fast Company*, and I'm responsible for the design of her feature. "Joy Meets World" is the headline. I turn the letters of "Joy" into two eyes and a nose, and curve "Meets World" to form a smiley face. On a deeper level, nods to the Japanese idea of cuteness, also known as kawaii. Design genius!

"Mike, I'm sorry, but I think this design is too playful for *Fast Company*," my editor in chief, Stephanie Mehta, tells me. So much for that design genius. She's right. The median age of our audience is in their forties, and this solution feels off base for them. Discouraged but not defeated, this error is like my first pancake: Tossed in the frying pan too quickly, it hasn't fully taken shape. I needed to think deeper about the audience, not myself.

Research turns up the heat when my ideas are cold. I uncover Kondo's elaborate organizational diagrams, which inspire a sophisticated design solution of letters folding like items of clothing. Months later, *Fast Company* snags a silver medal from the Society of Publication Designers for this feature—basically the Oscars of editorial design.

Harness your mistakes as opportunities to learn. Those specifics might take you somewhere unexpected.

Lean on Someone Else.

Photographer Peter Yang just wants the five-foot (1.5-m) disco ball to levitate. He's out in the middle of a field, on the set of a shoot with the electronic band Daft Punk for *Rolling Stone*. Every idea seems impossible, but then, Yang's prop stylist Spencer offers a simple suggestion: "What if they lean on the disco ball?" That was the shot. "Sometimes, you just set the scene and make people look cool in the photo," says Yang. When in doubt, simplify.

No.

Give Honest Feedback.

It might lead you to victory at the
U.S. Open, just like this graphic designer.

THE STAKES ARE HIGH FOR THE WORLD'S
most attended annual sporting event. Six thousand
ideas for the U.S. Open logo are scribbled on everything from utility bills, bank statements, and even
an airline menu. Sagi Haviv, the graphic designer
responsible for this logo, is determined to arrive at
the perfect solution. But despite his hours of effort,
only one logo will make the final cut.

The path to a great product is paved by honest
feedback. As a leader, that can be difficult—you may
not want to hurt your colleague's feelings—especially if you're a newly appointed to your position.
Don't sugarcoat it. Express what isn't working, and
explain *exactly* why. With murky feedback, you only
waste time and belabor the creative process.

Haviv demands excellence and needs decisiveness
from his team—not someone to tell him "the logos
are all good because you worked so hard," he says.

The winner? A reduction of the original U.S. Open
flaming ball symbol. While more drastic changes
were explored, and many looked great, "you need to
keep your feelings out of it and focus on what's best
for the client," says Haviv.

As a leader, remember: Your team looks to you for
guidance and direction. Lead them to create great
work, and they'll respect you for your honest feedback. They might even invite you to happy hour.

No.

⚡

**EASY
ENDURANCE
BOOST**

⊕

**WALK AND
MEDITATE**
If Marion Deuchars
needs a break
between illustration
assignments,
she'll go for a
head-clearing walk.
"I look at the trees or
listen to sounds,"
she says. When
having a hard time
staying present, she
recommends
game-ifying the
walk by looking for
one particular color
in the environment.
The activity will
occupy your brain.

▼
**Zakiya Pope,
on Creative Differences**
*"We all see the world through
our own lens. I think about
where the client is coming from,
and then walk them through my
journey to the final product."*

Make a Case for Your Work.

Especially if it involves a monkey.

CHERMAYEFF & GEISMAR & HAVIV never would've guessed a monkey could assist them with a logo redesign for Conservation International.

The organization wanted a new mark to represent their change in mission from environmental protection to world protection. Their original logo was a hand-painted logo of a jungle scene, complete with a beloved monkey hanging from a tree. "Could we add a human into this landscape?" the client asks.

However, Sagi Haviv has a different vision for the redesign. He presents a modernist archetype of a blue circle, with a green line underneath, symbolizing a blue planet on a green sustainable path.

"Are you crazy?" the client responds to his presentation. "We have this beautiful painting. And you're telling us to go with a circle and a line. What the hell does that mean?"

They agree to sit with it, but six months later, Haviv receives a call from the client. "People want the logo to have movement. A wave in the green line. Maybe a gradient? An arrow?" The client tries her hardest to retain the simplicity of the modernist logo.

And then, Haviv brings that monkey back.

The rational case of the modernist logo didn't work, so Haviv presents an emotional case. He places his favorite version of the logo onto videos that feature a monkey on a tree. *That* monkey.

They said yes. "It was magic," Haviv says.

Client isn't sold? Go full *Law and Order*, and make your case. Provide a logical and emotional rationale, and you'll reach a solution that satisfies everyone.

A FEEDBACK TRANSLATION GUIDE

How to turn confusing feedback into creative opportunities.

THEY SAY
"I'm not sure other people will get it."

YOUR PLAY
Walk through your creative process and how the solution is geared toward your end user.

THEY SAY
"This isn't what we discussed."

YOUR PLAY
Perhaps you made the work too polished too soon. Show them a sketch so they feel essential to the process.

THEY SAY
"Make it more fun!"

YOUR PLAY
Show images of outside work that is "more fun." Align on the definition so you don't make extra work for yourself.

THEY SAY
"Can I see a few more versions?"

YOUR PLAY
Ask questions about why this one isn't "it." The more specific, the fewer versions you'll need to make later on.

THEY SAY
"This is too out there."

YOUR PLAY
Don't overcorrect. Dial it back a little, and if that's still not enough, go for a more conservative approach.

Q + A

THE RACE CAR DRIVER

"OVERTHINKING GOES AGAINST YOU."
INSIDE THE MIND OF **HURLEY HAYWOOD,** THE UNDISPUTED CHAMP OF ENDURANCE RACING.

LOCATION
Jacksonville,
Florida

▼

FOR CREATIVES, THE ULTIMATE TEST of endurance is the all-nighter. We consume gallons of coffee and heaps of Kit-Kats to finish a project in time. But in the world of race car driving, there's an even greater challenge: the twenty-four-hour race. Drivers compete to cover the most miles on a grueling course that lasts a full day. Hurley Haywood is hands-down the best, having won 24 Hours of Daytona five times and Le Mans three times. In my interview with him, he shares his secrets for mental endurance and standing out in a crowd.

What's your key to endurance? Number one is focus. Racing is very much a mental exercise. You have to remain focused on the mission at hand.

Did you have a moment when you realized you had this gift of focus? No. I developed it over time. I didn't really know what I was doing at first. That's where my mentor Peter Gregg came into effect. He taught me to not make decisions irrationally. To make them on an educated basis rather than an emotional one.

Would you research other drivers before a race? Well, when I started, everything was new. There was no reference to other drivers. It was all about experience. You get better and better with more time on the track. Over time, a minute lap would take you fifty seconds.

What changes when you put your helmet on before a race? Your helmet is your shield. You're insulated from all of the things surrounding you. Concentrate 100 percent on getting the job done. The beginning of the race is when a lot of mistakes are made. Everybody's adrenaline is pushing to the maximum, and that's when people crash.

You seem like a patient guy. Being a race car driver is like playing chess. You've got to evaluate every single move on a success rate. If you're going to take a chance, and you have a 50/50 shot of making it correctly, that's a gamble. In long-distance racing, you can't afford to take a chance like that. In a regular workplace, there's a lot of leeway to make decisions.

Tell me about the first few minutes of a race. You start with a car that is mechanically as perfect as possible. But then the car's performance goes downhill. The tires and engine get hot. Track conditions change. You have to adapt to those changes. Quickly. Drivers that can't adapt don't succeed. You've got to be fluid in your evaluation of what's going on and make necessary adjustments.

Do you prefer a short sprint or a long race? A long-distance race gives you the opportunity to evaluate situations more carefully. In a sprint, you have one hour to get the job done. You have to evaluate the risk much quicker.

When I think about how that parallels design, I prefer a sprint. Too much time leads to overthinking. Neither of us can afford to overthink it. Overthinking goes against you. You don't want to spend too much time thinking about what you need to do to win. With experience, you can trust your moves and make decisions much quicker. If you spend too much time thinking about the opportunity, you lose it.

What does it feel like when the brakes give out? Your mind speeds up, but you can't follow your immediate reaction. I remember during Daytona in 2005, it was nighttime, and my brakes gave out right after a turn. I tried to pump them, but nothing was there. Instead of straightening the wheel, I turned it, and spun the car in the grass as much as I could before impact. That minimized the speed and damage. The more experience you have behind the wheel of a car, the better you handle urgent situations like these.

I watched your documentary, *Hurley*. You have a very understated personality. What's the value of that? You always want to have a surprise for somebody. When somebody has a misconception of you, you get on a racetrack and that all changes. It works on my behalf, not theirs. I don't try to be pretentious. I don't beat myself in the chest and say, "Hey, look at me!" I meld into the atmosphere and make the surprise move when somebody on the track is least expecting it.

 TAKEAWAYS

1 Research will enable you to make educated decisions when working quickly under high-pressure situations.

2 You don't need to oversell yourself, especially when stepping into a new job. Be understated, and let your work speak.

3 Think long, think wrong. Trust that your experience will lead you to the smart decision in a tough situation.

PLAN FOR A WRENCH

TWENTY-FOUR HOURS BEFORE the Grammys, wardrobe stylist Jeanie Cheek has a solid plan for Salt-N-Pepa's outfits. But then a text message from the creative producer, Fatima Robinson, throws a wrench into the works: "We can't use that houndstooth pattern. It'll clash." Salt-N-Pepa's outfits won't work with the houndstooth tracksuits that Cheek has planned for the backup dancers.

Be prepared for chaos, and look like a total pro at the Grammys.

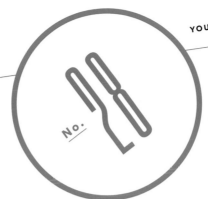

No.

CH

When you're working on a big project, how do you prepare for the unexpected? Let's look into Cheek's contingency plan.

"Okay. Give me a second." Unfazed, Cheek pulls out a forest green tracksuit with red-and-white stripes and shows it to Robinson. "Perfect," she replies.

Two weeks of planning enables Cheek to respond in that perfunctory "second." Armed with years of experience working on shows like *Lip Sync Battle* and the *BET Awards*, Cheek knows you need to over-prepare for the inevitable wrench that is flung into most of the projects.

Cheek purchased four different kinds of tracksuits, including the forest green ones that were chosen. "I'm like a duck that looks calm above water," she says, "but below, my legs are furiously working to keep things moving." She made that stressful "second" look effortless.

Despite the chaos, Cheek's driving force is the instant gratification of see-ing her work on stage and receiving feedback. At the end of the Grammys, a text message from Robinson pops up on Cheek's phone: "Great job."

Cheek's method of overplanning shares similarities with Olympian Billy Demong's practice of running on the treadmill for hours to ready himself for a half-hour sprint on the ski slopes. At the start of the next section, you'll discover preparation tactics to remain as cool as an astronaut during an interview at NASA.

MY GROWTH PLAN

"I try to connect as a human being."

—

WANT TO ILLUSTRATE A CHILDREN'S BOOK FOR KEVIN HART? JUST ASK **DAVID COOPER** HOW.

OCCUPATION
Illustrator,
Director of Photography

LOCATION
Maspeth,
New York

A COLLEAGUE FROM *Parents* magazine contacted me about a potential celebrity-driven project at Random House. Didn't know who. My rep and I thought it might be Spike Lee.

—

THEY GAVE ME ROUGH parts of the story. The guidelines were: The character needs to be pretty short, and his facial expressions need to be funny and over the top. Before I actually got picked for the project, I had to do some sample concepts.

—

THE BEGINNING OF every drawing feels like I'm doing it for the first time. Once I start, I know it's gonna suck, and I move past that. But then something clicks, and then I just keep drawing until it's done.

—

I DID AT LEAST twenty fully inked drawings,

drawing like this was already my project. I went into Random House and laid them all out on the table. Everyone appreciated how deep I went.

—

WHEN I FOUND out the project was about Kevin Hart, I thought, *Is this really happening?*

—

MARCUS WAS THE main character. In the first iteration, he had dreads and wasn't skinny. In the early stages, Kevin said, "Nah. You gotta clean up that hairline. You gotta taper that."

—

THERE WAS A lot of back-and-forth on the cover. At least eight rounds. Two months. But it's the most important part of the book.

—

I ORIGINALLY FOCUSED the cover on Marcus and one other character. They were holding one of those clapboards you see in movies. But Kevin had good feedback. He wanted to show Marcus with a community of diverse kids working together. I was worried it would look really crowded, but I made it work by putting Marcus in front and fanning out the other characters behind him.

—

IN THIS BOOK, Marcus started drawing a comic book to cope with his mother's death. He felt like he couldn't control anything in his life, and that comic was the only thing he could control. I really connected with that. I was going through something similar. My dad was dying of cancer.

—

THE DRAWINGS BECAME therapy for me.

—

MARCUS BATTLED a villain named The Doom, who personified cancer. I wanted the character to look soulless, so I gave him eyes that were slits, with flames coming out. His mouth was always open. He looked evil.

(**TAKEAWAYS**)

1
Pursue side gigs. One could turn into a new career.

2
Excited for a pitch? Give it your all, even if you're not sure if you'll score the job.

3
Not feeling creative in the beginning? Dealing with tough feedback from a client? It'll pass.

WE STARTED THE second book a few months after the first one. My drawings look way more confident—I had more fun with the compositions. I finished the cover in just two rounds.

—

DURING THE WHOLE process, the feedback never frazzled me. From working in magazines, I learned how to work with celebrities—everyone from Simone Biles to the Kardashians. Celebrities understand their image and have a lot of feedback. You have to respect that.

—

ILLUSTRATION WAS originally a side gig for me. I got my start as an assistant photo editor in the magazine industry. Admittedly, early in my career, I looked at being a photo editor as just a "job." But then, I made a decision to develop and balance both careers with intention.

—

I WORKED MY way up to photo director at one publisher over the course of seventeen years. One day, they let me go. They didn't lay out a red carpet at the door. It's just business.

—

I HAD TO DECIDE whether I'd stick with being a photo editor or try to be an illustrator full-time.

—

I CALLED MY literary agent and told him that I'd have a bit of free time. In a few months, he confirmed three illustration projects for me. The books and editorial projects work together to build financial stability.

—

MY DREAM PROJECT would be a children's book for Dwayne Johnson. I'd love to illustrate his life story from football to wrestling and acting.

—

PRESSURE DRIVES ME. I want to make this work. I'm gonna make this happen.

TAKEAWAYS

POWER-UPS
TO PLOW
THROUGH
YOUR NEXT
PROJECT.

Relate creative decisions to your end user. Give rational and emotional reasons why. → Research breaks creative blocks. → Simple goals for long-term focus. → Multiple prototypes for a surprising end result.

→ Atomize a big project into a bitsy checklist. Rapidly cross items off, and build momentum. Gratifying!

→ If client feedback makes the work better, then go for it. If it doesn't, show them an alternate version. → Make it look like it was done on purpose (even if it wasn't). → Murphy's Law: Whatever can go wrong, will go wrong. Plan for it. → Mistakes = learning. → But celebrate what went right, too!

ACTIVITIES

PUT YOUR
PROJECT
TO
THE TEST.

▸ **PUT YOUR
ERRORS
ON TRIAL**
P. 72

Reflect on a
previous project
where your
first idea didn't
work out.

What'd you learn
from the experience?

How did you apply
that learning to
the final product?

▸ **BEGIN WITH
RESEARCH.**
P. 54

Reading, interviewing, and creating polls are great
methods of research. Before you start your next project,
research for inspiration in the categories below.

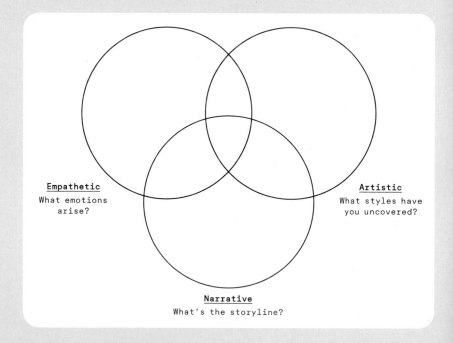

Empathetic
What emotions
arise?

Artistic
What styles have
you uncovered?

Narrative
What's the storyline?

▸ **JUST.
SAY. YES.**
P. 57

Manifest a dream
project, and keep
your ears open.

I want to make:

What's stopping you?

▸ SET SIMPLE GOALS. P.63

Let's plot out your next big project. What are your three main goals?

▸ BREAK BIG PROJECTS INTO SMALL PIECES. P.60

What are the key components that you can break a project into, and whom can you delegate them to?

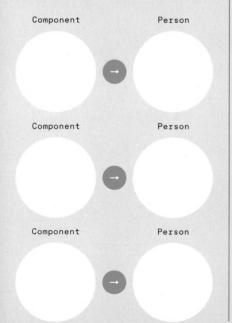

Component   Person

Component   Person

Component   Person

▸ THE CLIENT ISN'T ALWAYS WRONG. P.66

A quick pre-flight check before reacting to your client's feedback. They might be onto something.

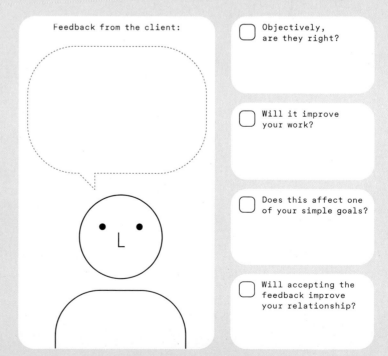

Feedback from the client:

Objectively, are they right?

Will it improve your work?

Does this affect one of your simple goals?

Will accepting the feedback improve your relationship?

Your Job

LAND THE PERFECT GIG, INTERVIEW LIKE A PRO, AND OVERCOME SELF-DOUBT.

▼ YOUR DAY

▼ YOUR PROJECT

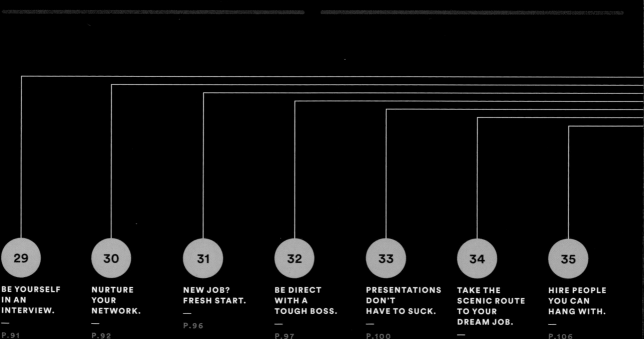

29

BE YOURSELF IN AN INTERVIEW.

—

P.91

30

NURTURE YOUR NETWORK.

—

P.92

31

NEW JOB? FRESH START.

—

P.96

32

BE DIRECT WITH A TOUGH BOSS.

—

P.97

33

PRESENTATIONS DON'T HAVE TO SUCK.

—

P.100

34

TAKE THE SCENIC ROUTE TO YOUR DREAM JOB.

—

35

HIRE PEOPLE YOU CAN HANG WITH.

—

P.106

INTERVIEWS

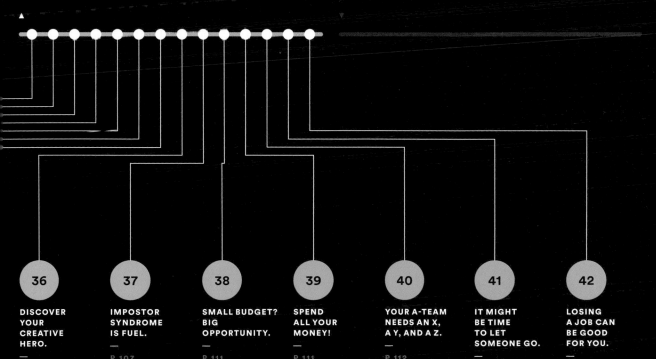

36

DISCOVER
YOUR
CREATIVE
HERO.
—
P.106

37

IMPOSTOR
SYNDROME
IS FUEL.
—
P.107

38

SMALL BUDGET?
BIG
OPPORTUNITY.
—
P.111

39

SPEND
ALL YOUR
MONEY!
—
P.111

40

YOUR A-TEAM
NEEDS AN X,
A Y, AND A Z.
—
P.112

41

IT MIGHT
BE TIME
TO LET
SOMEONE GO.
—
P.113

42

LOSING
A JOB CAN
BE GOOD
FOR YOU.
—
P.114

"If a design doesn't get deployed,

it's not the end of the world."

—ZAKIYA POPE

▼

P.105

29/Be Yourself in an Interview.

Zen and the art of scoring a dream job at NASA.

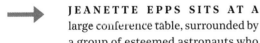 **JEANETTE EPPS SITS AT A** large conference table, surrounded by a group of esteemed astronauts who are unleashing rapid-fire interview questions, leaving Epps without time to think.

Interviews are nerve-wracking, to say the least.

As a creative director who regularly meets with job candidates, let me assure you: I don't want to see you fail. Let's have an honest chat so I can get to know the real you (while I take notes, of course). Be authentic—I'll have an easier time filling the blanks on the qualifications you don't have.

Epps's authenticity helps her land the job at NASA. "I was so relaxed because I didn't think they were going to select me," she says. This made the high-pressure interrogation feel like a series of casual conversations...with astronauts.

I use a similar (albeit more blunt) tactic when interviewing. "I don't care if I get this job" is my mantra. *Of course* I care, but this mantra reframes the high-pressure interview into a light chat. As a result, I act like myself and don't try to slip in vanilla-flavored buzzwords—those make me sound like everyone else.

Stand out by being yourself.

The key to a successful interview: Have a genuine conversation, and make a connection. Like any other relationship, this one needs to work both ways.

FOUR STEPS TO A STELLAR INTERVIEW

PREP YOUR QUESTIONS
Research the company. Ask about career growth. What are the necessary skills to be successful in this role? What's the culture like? Year-end reviews?

REHEARSE YOUR ANSWERS
Write them down, but don't read them verbatim. Say them out loud, reciting from memory, so they sound conversational. Grow comfortable with your answers.

DON'T TALK TOO MUCH
Get to the point. People notice soft answers. If you don't immediately have the answer, pause, and show that you're thinking. No need to rush.

FOLLOW UP
Send a thank-you note afterward. Always. Reference something that resonated, but don't go overboard. A sentence or two is enough to show you were engaged.

▼

**Vince Frost,
on Luck versus Effort**

*"Great opportunities have nothing
to do with luck. It's a lot of effort.
The more you put yourself out
there, the more you get in return."*

NURTURE YOUR

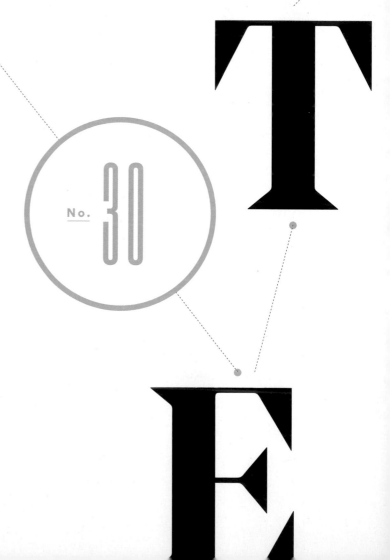

No. 30

IF YOU'RE A GRAPHIC designer named Bobby C. Martin Jr., you can manifest a dream job simply by giving someone a high-five.

Strolling through New York City one afternoon after lunch, Martin saw a familiar man striding toward him. As the distance closed between the two men, they simultaneously reeled their arms back, as if casting fishing rods, and slapped a high-five. "My man," said Martin to the stranger.

That stranger was none other than the mayor of Newark, Cory Booker.

Verbalizing your goals is the first step toward creating opportunities. "If Cory Booker ever runs to be president, I'd love to design his campaign," said Martin to Jennifer Kinon, his partner at Champions Design, a branding and graphic design firm. "I need to be careful what I say around Jennifer, because she'll make it happen," Martin told me.

A few kind words go a long way. Kinon shot an email to Michael Bierut, congratulating her former mentor on his win for the bid to design Hillary Clinton's logo.

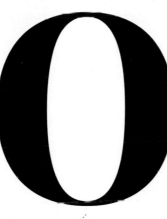

Turn hard work and a high-five into your dream job.

Minutes later, her phone rang. "You have to be the design director of Clinton's campaign," Bierut said to Kinon.

And so it happened. Kinon's words materialized an opportunity.

A few years later, Booker threw his hat into the presidential ring. Kinon tapped into her network—connecting with Booker's campaign manager, whom she worked with on Clinton's campaign.

And so, it happened, yet again. They scored Booker as a client. Martin's words coalesced into a design sprint where he and Kinon launched a branding system for Booker within weeks.

A sense of purpose fuels the designers through intense waves of work. "We do it because it's our responsibility," says Kinon. "Design can win an election and design can lose an election."

There's a historical thread to the art of manifestation. While at the School of Visual Arts, Kinon and Martin heeded the advice of Milton Glaser, the famed designer of the I Love NY logo. "Work be-gets work," he would often say. Once you do a great job on a project, you'll get hired for that type of work, again and again.

The throughline here? Let's say it out loud, together: Hard work. Again. Hard work. Once more, with gusto: Hard. Work.

 MY GROWTH PLAN

"Not everything is planned."

—

PETER YANG WAS ONCE A SHY KID, BUT THEN HE GREW UP AND PHOTOGRAPHED THE PRESIDENT.

OCCUPATION
Photographer

LOCATION
Los Angeles, California

M

MY MOM TAUGHT me to stand out. As an Asian immigrant in the American male-dominated field of computer engineering, she learned how to be seen.

—

SHE TOLD ME: "You're only going to talk when you think you have something important to say. Don't say anything." The first time I spoke in a meeting, I just agreed with my boss. It was so stupid, but I was proud of myself for speaking.

—

IN COLLEGE, my mom gave me a point and shoot camera for Christmas. I tried out to be the photographer for the school paper in Texas. I didn't know what the hell I was doing, but I was so passionate about photography.

—

I PHOTOGRAPHED THE Lonely Island guys

with Weird Al Yankovic for *GQ*. Everyone was wearing robes in a field of golden grass—shooting people in empty fields was big at the time. The Lonely Island guys were using these long straws to drink out of a massive punch bowl that Weird Al was holding.

—

THERE WAS A FALCON on set—it was one of my most ridiculous photo shoots. We tried to put a wig on the falcon, but it wasn't having it.

—

TO MAKE A CRAZY SHOOT like this work, I had to learn how to be forward and ask celebrities to do wild things. I would sketch out ideas and show the celebrity ahead of time. I didn't want to surprise them, so I always came prepared.

—

NOT EVERYTHING IS planned. When I photographed Will Ferrell for *Rolling Stone*, I said, "You're funny and people love you. Let's walk down the street and randomly meet people who want to take pictures with you."

—

WILL AND I WERE in New Orleans, during Mardi Gras. I rounded up a bunch of tourists and had them chase Will. The French Quarter is full of people. As he was running, he picked up this redheaded boy in a red shirt and red pants. The whole thing was absurd.

—

WHEN I PHOTOGRAPHED Senator Obama for *Rolling Stone*, I ran on adrenaline, joy, and a bit of fear. They wanted to pair him with a young photographer, so they hired me.

—

I WANTED TO MAKE the shoot different from what had already been done. I researched other magazine shoots of him. He looked very charismatic, but the photos felt very posed.

TAKEAWAYS

1
Sketch ideas ahead of time. Rough comps are easier to sell to a client than polished ones.

2
Planning is good. But if an unplanned idea pops up, and it's even better than what you planned, go for it.

3
Humor helps make high-pressure situations easier.

WHEN YOU HOLD the camera in front of your face, it's protection against having to engage with another human. I put my camera down and had a conversation with Obama.

—

WE WERE AT A FAIRGROUND. I made a joke about how it smelled like horseshit. I eventually got a great photo of him laughing for the cover. The most compelling moments are candid.

—

FOR YEARS, I WAS centered around shooting celebrity work. I couldn't make sense of how to shoot a noncelebrity in a compelling way, but then, the pandemic gave me a chance to reevaluate things. Nobody was commissioning photography. I needed to stay creative, so I photographed friends and family. This work was really meaningful—it came from inside. Now, Netflix uses these photos as reference for shoots they hire me for. These photos weren't originally shot to get more work; they were just for fun.

—

I LIKE TO DO OTHER things aside from photography to stay busy. I started taking Gaga dance lessons—they are in no relation to Lady Gaga. Gaga dance teaches you how to move your body in more advanced ways. I want to learn more about movement so I can better instruct my subjects on set.

—

THE ONE PERSON I wish I could photograph is Bruce Lee. As an Asian American, he was one of my role models. A marvel of physique, fashion, and attitude. I'd have him wear badass 1970s threads, bell bottoms and all.

—

I HAVEN'T HAD TO ASK my mom for money since my senior year of college in 1999. Shit, I just dated myself. Can you insert a part in here where Peter Yang takes a sip of his prune juice?

▼
Vaishnavi Mahendran, on That First Week of Work
"During my first week at Apple, I'd take the first shuttle to the office.
I could wander around and make it feel like it's my own space."

New Job?
Fresh Start.

You might even become
a YouTube star like this chef.

MOLLY BAZ'S HANDS ARE SHAKING as she sifts yolks for a batch of eggs Benedict. It's her first time being on camera for *Bon Appétit*.

Let's talk about firsts: Congrats on the new job! You made it through the interviews, the anticipation, the first day, the onboarding, the HR video, the icebreaker speech, and now...it's time to perform.

This is an opportunity to reinvent yourself. Your new boss will throw you into a big project: The Newbie Test. This could be a video, a piece of writing, an illustration. Don't worry, you're not going to fail. Nobody wants you to fail.

Well, except that one jerk. Prove 'em wrong.

BE GREAT ON CAMERA

DON'T SCRIPT IT
"It's never written word for word. That feels forced," says Baz. Bullet points ahead of time.

BE A COACH
Before filming, Baz tells herself, "You are not an actor. There's no reason to act differently."

START TALKING
Action! "Just open your mouth. Who you are is what needs to be on camera," says Baz.

No.
31

Think of it this way: Your boss doesn't want you to fail this test—they want to show off their new hire. They're behind you.

Welcome to Molly Baz's Newbie Test. *Bon Appétit* is experimenting with a new way of shooting food videos. Chefs joke around on camera. They interrupt cooking instructions to talk about songs on their playlists. They share earbuds. Their personalities are put on display, which makes them feel relatable, therefore the complex cooking techniques are easier to digest. But relatable isn't always easy. "It's the weirdest thing. When the camera is out in the test kitchen, everyone gets awkward," says Baz.

The camera rolls. And the first few words out of Baz's mouth are: "I'm kinda nervous!"

Bon Appétit decides not to edit this line out. This verdict shows conviction in Baz's relatability. "The comments on YouTube say things like, Oh my God, I love this Molly girl! More Molly! That reassurance really helped my confidence," says Baz. The millions of views on YouTube certainly don't hurt, either.

Baz makes a virtue out of acting imperfectly.

A new gig is a struggle. But you discover a new phase of your creativity through your response to that struggle. And you grow more confident and optimistic about the future. Why? Because you'll ace The Newbie Test. Over and over.

No.

Be Direct with a Tough Boss.

You won't get fired. Promise.

"DOES EVERYONE ON THE TEAM deserve to be here?" This loaded question was posed by the person who went on to become Eve Binder's boss at Chase Bank. They were hired...of course.

Bad bosses exist at all stages of your career. Luckily, the situation is temporary—one of you will eventually move on. Your best move while stuck together? Reframe it as a learning experience. Realize that these are behaviors to avoid once you become a leader.

Binder sharpened her skills in confrontational questioning. "When asked to do something I didn't agree with, I wouldn't ask why—that felt aggressive," she says. "Instead, I would ask, "What do you expect the impact to be?" This is a tool called the Socratic method you ask provocative questions to stimulate critical thinking. It helped Binder understand her bosses' motivations and solve their thorny problems.

This bad-boss experience helped Binder flourish as a leader. In her current role as senior design manager at Grubhub, she reframes prescriptive comments from executives, such as "I want you to do this," into exciting opportunities, such as "How can we make this moment feel more celebratory?" This gives her team members a chance to formulate their own solutions and become more invested in the final product.

For every after-hours emailing, credit-stealing, gaslighting boss, there's an opportunity to learn what *not* to do once you're the person in charge.

MANAGE YOUR MANAGER

A field guide to taming all types of bosses.

THE MICRO-MANAGER
Problem: They want to be a part of every step of your creative process.
Solution: Specify exactly what you'd like feedback on so it doesn't get unwieldy.

THE TRANSIENT
Problem: They give you wishy-washy feedback.
Solution: Set regular check-ins, and create a shared document of your goals. Refer back to those goals during your check-ins.

THE SCORCHER
Problem: They're sarcastic and shred your work to bits.
Solution: Get personal. Tell them it feels deflating. They may see it in a different way, as if they are being humorous.

THE REBEL
Problem: They want to change the company overnight.
Solution: Offer insights into other coworkers in the office and how they might be able to help.

THE YOUNG ONE
Problem: They have less experience than you.
Solution: Explain the inner workings of the office, processes that could improve, and seek their fresh perspective.

Q

+

A

THE OLYMPIC GOLD MEDALIST

"I SUCKED IN HIGH SCHOOL."
BILLY DEMONG RECOUNTS THE
VALUE OF HARD WORK AND
HAVING A COUNTERTOP BUSINESS.

LOCATION
Park City,
Utah

▼

A SKIER ROCKETS INTO THE AIR AT 60 mph (97 kph), hits the ground, and propels into a cross-country ski race. This is Nordic combined skiing, a sport which Billy Demong made history for the United States by winning Olympic Gold in 2010. Demong's historic win is the result of determination, but also a creative training plan that involves unconventional workouts such as cycling and running backward on a moving walkway. To gain insight into the mental toughness required to succeed as an Olympian, I spoke with the intrepid skier himself.

As a kid, what did you want to grow up to be? I thought I wanted to be a pilot. I started applying to the Air Force Academy, but then things turned around. I started dreaming and setting goals for the 2002 Olympics. Physically, it might've been possible at that age, but mentally, it wasn't. I finally won my fourth Olympics in Vancouver in 2010 after dialing in my recipe for endurance.

What's your recipe for endurance? A coach once told me: "Kansas is boring, but you can't get to Colorado unless you drive through Kansas." The things you need to do to become great can be very boring and methodical.

How do you feel about the idea of talent? People put too much emphasis on it. It takes away from hard work. I sucked in high school. I had to work really hard to figure it all out. And that meant thinking about nutrition, training, and recovery. Incessantly. It also meant figuring out how to rest and live a sustainable life.

What's creative about skiing? You can create any training plan to execute. My favorite process was figuring out how to stack workouts. I had to be flexible and creative. It didn't matter if I got stuck in an airport. I'd run backward on a moving walkway to get a workout in.

What was the toughest feedback you ever received? While training for the Olympics, I was also racing bikes. I had a coach who didn't understand—he was new. I knew cycling would make me worse, because I'd lose some flexibility in the beginning. But in the long run, it would make me stronger. This coach pulled me aside and said: "Because you raced bikes all summer, you will fail. You're too heavy for ski jumps." I went onto the best start of a season in the overall World Cup lead after the first few events.

Do you think his feedback was part of the reason for your success? I definitely fed off it. I like proving people wrong. I like being an underdog. It was actually hard for me to stay on top. Once I was on top, it became boring. I was like, all right, let's go find something else to work on now.

What was your favorite job aside from skiing? When I retired, I led a national leadership organization, USA Nordic Sport, for two Olympic cycles. I loved building an organization and its revenue streams. Now, I don't want to rush into another CEO role. I want to reset and figure out what I'm going to do for the next twenty years. What's going to make me happy is important for my sustainability.

You've had a lot of jobs. What are the mental benefits of learning multiple skills? Like anyone who becomes good at something, over time athletics gets easier. You can refine your craft, but you can't spend more time on it. That leaves you with free time to occupy yourself. Back in the days of distance learning, I was living in a chicken coop. I would order books on hunting, fishing, investing, and carpentry. For about six months, I'd focus on the learning phase, but then I needed hands-on experience to really understand a new skill. At one point, I even had a countertop business.

What was your favorite side gig? I would absolutely say carpentry. It was really satisfying and mentally clearing. Devices would go away, unless needed for research. You work with a team to problem solve, build something together, and at the end of the day, you see what you accomplished.

Is it hard for you to sit still right now? (Laughs) No, we're doing something. We're talking. It's mentally stimulating. I do need to have a plan. I need to know that tomorrow is going to be busy. But as I get older, I definitely need to take more naps.

TAKEAWAYS

1 Diligence is stronger than talent. Success comes to those willing to put in the hours of hard work.

2 Prove the doubters wrong. If someone says "you can't," work harder to prove to them that you can.

3 Set a plan, and follow it. Consistency is key, especially when you're not motivated. Knock it off your checklist. You'll feel better.

▼
KeiVarae Russell, on Preparation
*"Watching film of the other team before a big game would boost my
confidence and eradicate stress, because I felt like I did my homework."*

33/Presentations Don't Have to Suck.

Lessons from an inspirational speaker's tough crowd of coal miners.

 STANDING BEFORE A ROOM OF soot-covered coal miners who've just completed a twelve hour shift, the inspirational speaker Dick Beardsley delivers a presentation about his career as a runner. These hard workers just want to go home. "There was no response. No one laughed. Nothing," he reflects.

As Beardsley knows, delivering a great presentation is an essential skill, and you need to understand how to engage the audience, whether they are fellow creatives, prospective clients, or tired coal miners.

"I ignore the crowd and think back to a presentation where they went wild," says Beardsley. He uses a reframing tactic called false motivation to keep himself fired up. This tool is also useful on a video call, when your confidence is smoldering because the audience has turned their screens off.

There are tricks to boost your mood. Smile and use an uplifting tone when you speak. Focus on those who express interest, even if it's just a few folks. Your confidence will boost, and so will the number of engaged audience members.

Beardsley connects by using personal tales that excite him. "Even though it may not be exactly what the audience went through, they can relate, because it's a real life story," he says.

In short: Have fun. Your audience will too.

A CREATIVE KEYNOTE UNLOCKED

 DO THIS   **NOT THAT**

⊘ **REHEARSE** The more familiar you are with the slides, the less jittery you'll feel on presentation day.	⊗ **OVERREHEARSE** You'll worry about forgetting your speech, and that added stress will stiffen you up.
⊘ **SET AN AGENDA** Let people know what to expect. Clarify that questions can be asked at the end.	⊗ **MIDWAY Q&A** If you feel the need to stop to take questions, your deck might be too long. Cut a slide or two.
⊘ **KNOW YOUR CROWD** Creatives love sketches, process, and a short personal story to prove a point.	⊗ **NAVEL-GAZE** Business folk want to get right to it. Don't harp on your mood board for too long.

"**I'M PROMOTING SOMEONE ELSE.** Sorry, man." David Curcurito tells me about the potential job at *Esquire*. "But I can make you deputy art director," he says, as a consolation prize.

We're standing in a bar adorned with dark wood and maroon, which feels like an appropriate setting to receive a job offer from one of the most esteemed men's magazines on the planet. Until moments ago, I was confident the invitation meant I was about to score the coveted position of art director and would be second in command. One step closer to leadership.

But...no.

Curcurito's offer hangs in the air like a plume of smoke. I hoist my whiskey glass to my mouth to build in a natural pause as his words settle in.

Deputy? I feel like the graphic design version of a mall cop. *Deputy?* Does a badge come with this title? I pause, letting my ego get it all out of its system. I'm not going to let a title get in the way of the job of my dreams. *Of course* I'll take the job.

Promotions and new jobs won't always come as quickly as you'd like—in fact, your career will flow at the pace of stop-and-go traffic on the world's longest road trip. Enjoy the slow path. It's an opportunity to hone your skills.

TAKE THE SCENIC ROUTE

 AN EXTREME STORY TO HELP YOU THROUGH A TOUGH JOB

In the blistering heat of White Sands, New Mexico, Noah Galloway embarks on the Bataan Memorial Death March, a grueling Spartan Race that pushes athletes to their very limits. Hiking 26.2 miles (42 km) while wearing a 50-pound (23-km) backpack is difficult enough, but as an extra challenge, Galloway wears a mask that cuts off 25 percent of his oxygen. Currently struggling with dehydration, nausea tempts him to consider stripping the mask off. But why do this? Galloway admits his appetite for extreme challenges stems from an

DREAM JOB.

In my case, I need to rebuild my creative engine, and...it's gonna be a while.

My go-to design tricks no longer work at *Esquire*. The magazine takes an innovative approach to storytelling through words and visuals—it's a gordian knot of art direction, and to untangle it, I must relearn my craft. For a year, I churn out some seriously lousy design work.

Things turn around.

"Dude, I think you finally figured it out," Curcurito says to me during my exit interview, one year later. "It's too bad you're leaving now!"

The title of my next job, wait for it...deputy art director. At *Men's Health*.

During marathon training, you push your body harder and harder by gradually running farther distances.

TO YOUR

The unbearable lightness of waiting for the right gig.

Muscle fibers shred, proteins flood the fissures. I was suddenly a stronger designer. *Men's Health* content is certainly more low-brow (see: beer, barbells, and buffalo wings), but I spark it with sophistication, using what I learned at *Esquire*.

I'm shocked. I feel comfortable from the very beginning at *Men's Health*. The work I created at *Esquire* wasn't as much of a car crash as I thought. For the next four years, I fine-tune my design aesthetic and leadership skills as I climb to second in command of *Men's Health*.

Six years later, while driving through the steel gray plateau of Iceland, on the tail end of a much-needed respite from my new job at *Popular Science* (yes, another deputy title), a career-changing message pops up on my phone. "Interested in applying to be the creative director for *Men's Health*?" The stoplight of my career turns green, and I race forward.

Your career isn't a race to the top. It's a journey filled with pit stops that are opportunities to learn and grow. Don't be discouraged by less-than-prestigious job titles or low pay. Focus on your developments, and before you know it, your career will accelerate faster than expected.

---

injury that left him a double amputee. "I didn't know if I still had what it takes to push myself past those limits, so I started signing up

for Spartan Races," he says. Galloway finishes the race and ends up in the emergency room. "I outlasted eighty able-bodied

people," he reflects. "That was a powerful moment. What else am I capable of?" When you're struggling at a job, whether it's a

tough boss, a new skill, or a culture you're still adapting to, remember: You have the ability to endure far beyond what you believe.

 MY GROWTH PLAN

"Failing doesn't mean I'm a failure."

—

SITTING ON THE BENCH DURING
HER FRESHMAN YEAR OF VOLLEYBALL MADE
ZAKIYA POPE A BETTER DESIGNER.

OCCUPATION
Senior Behavioral Designer-
Vice President, U.S. Bank

LOCATION
New York,
New York

WESTERN MICHIGAN UNIVERSITY called to say I was nominated for the Volleyball Hall of Fame back in 2016. I thought they were calling me to pay some outstanding parking tickets.

—

I WAS BENCHED my entire freshman year as a volleyball player at Western Michigan University. To make it on the team, I had to run a mile (1.6 km) in six minutes and forty-five seconds, but I wasn't able to go that fast. I would call my mother crying every morning before we had to run.

—

THE SETBACK TAUGHT me patience, and to not worry about output. Focus on the process and the learnings.

—

JUST SHOWING UP was the biggest hurdle to overcome, but I was committed to my team.

WHEN I RETURNED for preseason my sophomore year of volleyball, everything on the court clicked. I didn't have to think about my footwork, arm swing, or timing—my coach instilled those fundamentals during my freshman year.

—

AT CHASE BANK, my team worked on an innovative project called Finn—an experience for everyday people that didn't have a ton of money. Not only the 1 percent. An app that would help those people spend their money more wisely.

—

WE PITCHED A FEATURE that would aggregate all of a user's spending and then categorize it into a visual diagram. A user could assign emotions to different parts of their spending. They could say that spending money on coffee brought them joy.

—

FOR OUR PRESENTATION to the C-suite, we walked them through scenarios of different types of people using this app. We explained how valuable this would be for a college student in debt.

—

CHASE MEASURES the revenue associated when they decide to greenlight a project. Finn was geared toward people with lower balances in their account. The project fizzled.

—

IT DIDN'T FEEL GOOD. Our team put in a lot of work, research, and we really fought for what we believed in.

—

ULTIMATELY, I DIDN'T feel like a failure because of it. I grew more confident about telling a story and presenting a case for the body of work that we produced. I learned how to conduct research and show users how to use new features. The project wasn't well received at first, but that doesn't mean it wasn't good work.

TAKEAWAYS

1
Project didn't launch? Bummer. Components of the project (such as an icon set) launched? Great. Put those in your portfolio.

2
Patience is key to growth. Focus on what you learned versus what failed.

3
Keep showing up. You'll get better.

IF A DESIGN DOESN'T get deployed, it's not the end of the world.

—

YEARS LATER, CHASE USED an automated savings feature that we created. You can round up a purchase so it puts the leftover change into a savings account. Spend $4.50 on a coffee, and it'll save the change. It felt great to see how they used valuable pieces.

—

WHILE IT WAS A FAILURE from a product standpoint at first, it was a success in the long run. It just depends on how you look at it and what your benchmark for success is.

—

VERY FEW THINGS in life happen instantly. Working in the field of finance, projects take a long time.

—

I WANT TO MAKE AN IMPACT. There's a lot of irrational behavior around money and spending. A majority of the population are confused about investing, saving, and even health care. Design can help democratize it.

—

THE NEXT THING I want to tackle is the design of forms. You have to fill out a form for everything you do. You can't open up a bank account or apply for school without filling out a form. They're a necessary evil. But like, why do they still look so bad? They need to be redesigned to be less confusing, and I think that humanity will thank us for it.

—

I USED TO RARELY look back at my contributions. When I was inducted into the Hall of Fame, I was surprised at what I had accomplished and how good it made me feel years later. The homesick, crybaby freshman who wanted to quit made it into the history books.

▼
Jay Osgerby, on Collaboration
"Every good partnership needs an accelerator and a brake. At our design studio, I'm the accelerator—constantly looking for new work. My partner, Ed, wants to have fewer projects, but focus more. We're yin and yang."

No.

35

Hire People You Can Hang With.

This celebrity author rewrites the script on interviewing with authenticity.

INTERVIEWS CAN BE A STRANGE transaction. In just an hour, a candidate must put on their best performance, while you decide if they're the right fit. Neil Strauss is expert-level, having interviewed everyone from Lady Gaga to Taylor Swift. He shares his tips on how to unlock your interviewee's authentic self.

1. Avoid objectifying the person. While interviewing the musician Chuck Berry, Strauss steered clear of standard-fare questions about rock 'n' roll. "Chuck just wanted to laugh," says Strauss.

2. Research everything. Strauss will do his homework on the person and write up to ten pages of questions. He studies them right before the interview and then throws them out. This allows conversation to flow naturally—the questions are in Strauss's head.

3. Plan your first question. "It sets the tone," says Strauss. "It can't be so vague that it seems like you know nothing about the person. It also can't be so specific that it seems like you're obsessed with them."

4. Don't read off a list of questions. It ruins the potential connection you could make. Ask questions based on curiosity.

5. Prepare to scrap your plan. During an interview for *NME* magazine, Julian Casablancas of The Strokes continued to turn off Strauss's tape recorder. "As a writer, my goal is to really understand what makes someone tick," says Strauss.

When you're a hiring manager, it's important to put your potential employee at ease so their personality can shine. Make an effort to understand their motivations, and they'll work harder for you.

Discover Your Creative Hero.

No.

36

DESIGNER MICHELLE DOUGHERTY'S MENTOR AT IMAGINARY FORCES WAS KYLE COOPER, WHO CREATED CHILLING TITLES FOR MOVIES SUCH AS *SEVEN*. "HE WAS INTO SHAKESPEARE AND STORYTELLING. SO INSPIRING. I DIDN'T LEARN ABOUT THAT IN SCHOOL," SHE SAYS. "HE'S THE REASON I DO WHAT I DO."

No. 37

Impostor Syndrome Is Fuel.

And it can help you
score a big promotion, just
like this art director.

"FOR A LONG TIME, I FELT LIKE A FAILURE AT MY JOB," says Jaspal Riyait about her role at *The New York Times.* "It's such a prestigious place—the best of the best work there." ¶ Similar to Riyait, you landed your dream job because you're talented, but you may not believe in yourself—the paradox of impostor syndrome **(1)**. It's a powerful tool when you reframe it as a force to learn and grow. Riyait didn't let impostor syndrome hold her back. She took courses in video editing and coding. She listened to health and wellness podcasts. She pitched stories to editors **(2)**, which is uncommon practice for an art director. (Traditionally, editors will create the stories, and art directors visualize them.) Riyait flipped the script. ¶ Her defining project was titled What Loss Looks Like, a moving virtual memorial for the pandemic of 2020. The project invited *The New York Times* readers to submit photographs of objects that reminded them of their loved ones who had passed away. "It was an emotional story that everybody could connect to," Riyait says. She earned a coveted byline in *The New York Times* and was eventually promoted to senior editor. Riyait's impostor syndrome propelled her out of the comfort zone and into an exciting new position.

1

PERCEPTION

Their Skills

Your Skills

It's natural to believe others are more skilled. But there's a difference between skills and familiarity. Your new colleagues have greater familiarity with the company.

2

REALITY

Their Skills

Your Skills

Your distinct viewpoint holds value, especially where colleagues have adhered to the status quo. Because it was done one way doesn't make it the right way.

THE FITNESS INFLUENCER

MASSY ARIAS'S SCHEDULE IS MORE HECTIC THAN TETRIS ON THE HIGHEST LEVEL. HOW TO MAXIMIZE YOUR CREATIVE OUTPUT LIKE HER.

LOCATION
Los Angeles,
California

MASSY ARIAS IS AN ENTREPRENEUR who runs seven self-funded businesses, including personal training and a line of all-natural supplements. Despite her busy schedule, she stays connected with her millions of Instagram followers through a steady stream of health and wellness content. She remains calm and balanced, thanks to her ability to understand her creative patterns. Arias knows when to push hard, but also the value of enjoying downtime to be fully present with her daughter. Here's what we can learn from her about work-life balance.

Talk me through a typical day of yours. I'm a single mom, and I'm responsible for a lot. I woke up at 5:30 a.m. today. I get up early so I can connect with my East Coast team at a decent time. After our meeting, work has been delegated, and they know exactly what they need to do. We'll have a call at 1:30 p.m. to catch up. Right now, my daughter is in the living room, because she's off from school. I'm keeping her entertained. I'll drive an hour and forty-five minutes to the office to meet a client of mine and film content with her.

How do you get it all done? I wake up early. No excuses. This is a busy season of my life, and I have to push through. This is not going to be forever. Once my daughter goes into middle school, it'll be a little bit easier. I do whatever is needed to accomplish my goals. I know that when I'm getting a lot from one area of my life, other areas are not going to be perfect.

How do you remain creative while stressed? The mistakes I made were because I didn't have enough organization in my life. Now, I look at the year ahead and plan for the busy seasons. The holidays are what I call the Super Bowl of fitness. That's when I need to generate a lot of content. As of right now, we've shot absolutely everything for the next sixteen weeks.

Part of your strategy is to plan ahead. Nobody talks about the fact that when you're creating all of this content, you're not *really there* with your kid. I'm a single parent, and when I have my daughter, I need to be present for her. If it's my turn to take care of her, and I need to pick her up from school, my day ends at 3 p.m.

Do you find algorithms to be creatively stifling? When it comes to health and wellness, things can be very superficial. I don't follow trends.

You do your thing. We do polls and ask questions on social media. That's how we base our content. But I have to connect with it. Right now, people are feeling stressed during the holidays. And so am I. My video guy and I sit together, have a conversation, and create content. But I also give facts, because people are seeking the truth. I teach what stress is, why it decreases motivation levels, and how that affects you physically.

How else are you creative? Many people don't know this, but I used to sing as a soprano for Bloomberg's New York City Choir. I sang all throughout high school. I'm very extroverted and love to perform. I love people. My parents saw me

as a leader from a young age. But it's funny. Professionally, I was afraid of speaking in public, so I took media training. I was having trouble finding the words, because I have a bilingual brain. I was using all these "ums" in between words. I'm like, "I know what I'm talking about."

You speak very confidently. Tone is important when I'm training a client—it emulates a different response in people. You can be creative with tone and change it depending on the emotion you're looking for. No one is going to take me seriously if I'm talking in a high pitch (changes pitch).

Did you grow up in New York City? I came at a very young age. It was rough. I was in situations where I had to figure out myself, but my parents had trust in me. They put a lot of pressure on me. Good pressure. My dad used to say, "I always knew you'd be an entertainer."

It seems like you do well under pressure. I want to be in the fire every day. It keeps me alive. I love a challenge, because I know what comes at the end. I know that I can get through it.

TAKEAWAYS

1 Look ahead, and plan for your busy seasons at work. Conserve energy for sustainable creative output.

2 Connect with your audience. Polls on social media and feedback forms will tell you what's working. And what isn't.

3 Speak with confidence when you present work. But don't oversell it, and be vulnerable when you don't have an answer.

SMALL BUDGET? BIG OPPORTUNITY.

No.

38

Your budget is as thin
as a roll of one-ply toilet paper.
Wipe the floor with it.

VINCE FROST IS carefully constructing a miniature city with letterpress spacers, caddy cornering the pieces to form the word "Big" in a bold, condensed typeface. This typographic cover for *Big Magazine* is one of the art director's first assignments since his departure from the design firm Pentagram.

Big Magazine, a renowned art and culture magazine, was a dream for any guest art director to work on. Freedom to redesign a publication with an audience in fashion, art, and advertising. Globally focused content that ranges from stories on Cape Town, Madrid, and even Route 80 in the United States. The downside: a tight budget.

"I need limitations to be creative," says Frost. "If a client gives me complete freedom, I'm terrified." The lack of funds focuses Frost's eye on the weathered letterpress spacers, seeing them as metaphors for city blocks.

Frost's inventive typographic solution cements his career in the editorial world. *Time* and *Vogue Japan* hire Frost for assignments, as they assume he's a seasoned magazine art director based on his work. "Truth is, I didn't know how to do it. I just had to do it," he reflects. The excitement of the opportunity fueled Frost through the projects.

This example shows how small projects can lead to bigger jobs. "If I said no, I wouldn't have such great opportunities in my life," says Frost. Today, he runs Frost*collective, a design studio of forty-plus people in Australia.

Next time the funds are scarce, get crafty. This might be your *Big* opportunity.

Spend All Your Money!

—

"The plan was for Nick Kroll do a full split, while jumping in the air," says photographer Peter Yang. "I was very insistent on a fitted suit, because that would make it funnier." Kroll was photographed for *GQ* in an old motel, which saved money but added a layer of kitsch to the concept. Save where you can, but don't skimp on the essentials, like Kroll's suit. Remember: Spend your entire budget every year. If you don't, it could get slashed.

No.

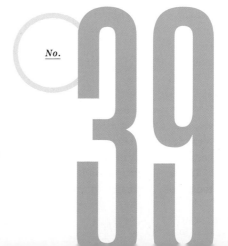

▼
KeiVarae Russell, on Great Coaching
"When I was on the Green Bay Packers, defensive back coach Jerry Gray catered to the style of the individual players. That got the best out of us."

Your A-Team Needs an X, a Y, and a Z.

Lessons learned from experts on the racetrack and the volleyball field.

WITH SIX MINUTES LEFT IN THE RACE and barely any fuel in the tank, race car driver Leh Keen was in danger of losing Sahlen's Six Hours of the Glen. "I knew that it was not going to make it," his partner Andrew Davis told the *Florida Times-Union.*

The two drivers are polar opposites. Davis is analytical. Keen just wants to drive fast. But in this race, his strategy paid off. By stretching a tank of gas for fifty-two minutes, he earned a two-lap lead, and won.

This duo was paired by endurance driving legend Hurley Haywood, who understands the value of a balanced team. "Place individuals where their personalities excel, but they still work as a unit," he says.

Diversity is essential for success. Zakiya Pope, senior behavioral designer-vice president at U.S. Bank, stresses the importance. With a diverse team, members don't need to "code-switch with one another," she says. "That boosts emotional security and provides mental and emotional endurance."

Diversity had a strong influence while Pope was a volleyball player at Western Michigan University. Initially, she was one of three Black players, but two years later, half of the team was Black. "After my career ended, I met Black women who started playing because they saw themselves in our team," she says.

Take steps toward building a more diverse team today, and you'll engineer a more diverse tomorrow.

No.

EASY
ENDURANCE
BOOST

SNAG A POWER NAP
Switching between tasks like writing, illustration, and lettering can be mentally draining for Marion Deuchars. She utilizes fifteen-minute naps to hit the reset button. "I can sleep on a bed of concrete. It really doesn't matter," she says. When Deuchars shared a studio with other artists, they kept a mattress on-site.

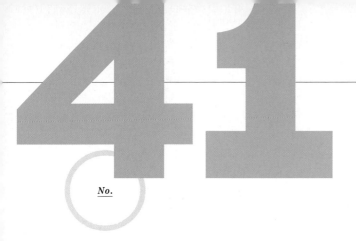

No.

It Might Be Time to Let Someone Go.

Firing isn't fun, but the person might actually thank you for it.

AFTER I FIRED THIS PERSON, THEY shook my hand.

Before I started the job, a lot of negative things were said about them. I wanted to be fair, give them a chance, and form my own opinion before making any rash decisions. When we first met, they were charming. Talented. Excited about my direction for the magazine. I felt conflicted about what I heard.

As a leader, you'll face similar conflicts around hiring and firing. Lesson number one: Decisions need to be made in the best interest of the team dynamic.

My team dynamic was on the decline.

Thump. Thump. They drag their feet as they come in late one morning. Hey, I can tolerate lateness. As long as the work gets done, and the lateness is occasional, all is good. Clunk. Clunk. They drop their feet on the desk like a child dropping their backpack on the floor after a long day of school. I ask them to kindly remove their feet. They refuse.

This is the moment I decided to fire them.

Actions like these made my team uncomfortable, and I sensed that was affecting their creativity.

Once we severed ties, the person complimented my leadership style as being "incisive." I was surprised and felt better about my tough call.

While my decision slowed down production in the short term, I made a great hire who lifted the mood and boosted morale in the long run. Happy employees make great things.

As a leader, it's important to make decisions that benefit the team as a whole. Let that one jerk go.

 TROUBLESHOOT A TOUGH TEAM MEMBER
A map for improvement before you decide to hit the eject button.

 THEY'RE SLOW
Give them time to improve—you weren't always this quick. Set them up with a midlevel person on your team who can share knowledge with them.

 THEY COMPLAIN
"How can I help you solve this?" is a question that will turn complaining into action. Be clear on business goals, and clarify that some problems are unavoidable.

 THEY DON'T TAKE FEEDBACK
Wait for multiple incidents, and comment on an overall trend. Help them see your vision, but also be direct about what you want. You're the manager.

 THEIR WORK IS SUBPAR
But they had such a great portfolio! Learn about their previous boss— that person might've had a heavy hand in their work. Provide attainable goals.

 THEY JUST DON'T GET IT
Offer training. Review the job description to clarify what's expected. Make a clear plan on how to improve. Firing shouldn't come as a surprise.

▼
**KeiVarae Russell,
on Anticipation**
*"Being a free agent in the NFL is tough, but I
can only control so much in life. I stay in shape
and stand ready to go when a team calls."*

A reinvention plan for when you get laid off. But first: karaoke!

I TOOK THE DOG FOR A WALK, sat down on a park bench, and cried. The email from the human resources department landed like a grenade in my inbox: "Meeting at 10 a.m." I knew my job as creative director at *Men's Health* would be incinerated in an hour.

My first leadership position was also my first job loss. "What'd I do wrong?" repeated in my head. In the world of magazines, we identify ourselves with our workplaces (not healthy, I know). Eve would joke and call me Mr. Men's Health. I no longer had a job.

Who was I?

After that fateful meeting with human resources, I enjoyed one of the best nights of karaoke with my art department and waved goodbye to my past. This was an opportunity to rethink who I was.

Still a magazine creative director?

Or more?

As you learned in the very beginning of this book: Start Moving, Keep Moving. This applies to a job loss. Regular visits to former coworkers kept my endorphin levels high, but they *really* spiked when I popped into the *Entertainment Weekly* office on a whim. The design director literally just quit. That day. Quick takeaway: If you continually put yourself out there, a great opportunity will appear.

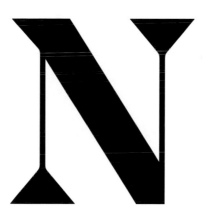

I N G

A JOB CAN
BE GOOD FOR YOU.

Entertainment Weekly offered me a freelance gig, as well as a chance to reconnect with Henry Goldblatt, the editor in chief. He had some great intel: *Fast Company* was on the hunt for a creative director, and his former colleague, Stephanie Mehta was the newly minted editor in chief of this revered publication.

Thanks to a glowing recommendation from Henry, I landed an interview for the creative director position.

It was show time.

The meeting with Stephanie was uplifting. It didn't feel like an interrogation. Instead, it was a smooth conversation, where I sensed her trust in me—that trust is crucial for a strong creative partnership. This was a great opportunity. I busted my ass through follow-up interviews and a rigorous visual analysis of *Fast Company*'s presence in print, web, social media, awards, and events.

Victory. Four months after my first job loss, I was employed again.

Losing my job at *Men's Health* smashed me to pieces, but the hardship gave me an opportunity to rebuild myself. I've grown into a creative director who oversees not only a magazine, but the entire *Fast Company* brand.

Yes, you too will lose a job at some point in your career. Reframe it as the end of a chapter, not the end of a book, and you'll write an even more exciting story.

There are many tools at your disposal to craft a life-long narrative. In the next and final section, you'll learn how a graphic designer taps into her South Asian culture, a nine-year old taps into her imagination, and a seventy-six-year-old painter and poet proves that it's never too late to start a new chapter of life.

NO. 42

→ MY GROWTH PLAN

"I gave them the courage to fly."

HOW PROFESSOR **ANGELA RIECHERS** USES HISTORY TO INSPIRE HER STUDENTS TO MOVE FORWARD.

OCCUPATION
Program Director, Graphic Design
University of the Arts

LOCATION
Philadelphia,
Pennsylvania

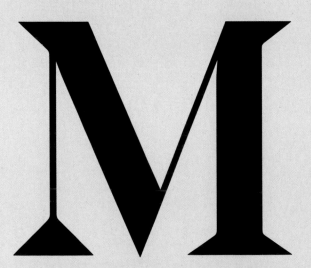

M

MY BOXING GLOVES were custom-made by a guy in the Bronx. Beautiful black-and-gray leather.

—

IN 1993, I BELONGED to Gleason's Gym in Brooklyn. My boxing trainer was Martin Snow; he was on *The Real Housewives of New York*. Big, goofy-looking guy who is super smart, emotionally intelligent, and full of Zen master sayings. He used to randomly go out into the street outside his gym and throw a football to the guys in the fire truck. They'd always catch it.

—

IN 1995, THERE WAS going to be a Golden Globes competition for women in Madison Square Garden. I was supposed to be in it. But then I got pregnant with my son and had to drop out.

—

THE END OF MY TIME in magazines was

particularly tough, and I was going through serious family issues. My second-to last job was great: a wonderful art department, an editor in chief who was fully supportive of the design vision. Great stories, great budgets. We did beautiful, award-winning work. Then the editor left and the design directors got replaced. Things changed.

—

MY BOSS AT MY FINAL JOB was terrible. I once broke a tooth while eating a bagel at work and needed to rush out for an emergency root canal. My new boss required me to come back that afternoon after the procedure.

—

WITHOUT GRIT I WOULD not have survived my boss. I went to the gym every morning, and I ran on the treadmill. I hate running. I kept telling myself, "Tougher than you know, tougher than you know, tougher than you know."

—

A BIKE MESSENGER once patted me very gently on the shoulder and said "You'll get better." New Yorkers can be so great to one another.

—

I WAS SURROUNDED by people that were better designers than me. I'm a better teacher and writer than I am a designer. I'm okay with that.

—

THE FIRST CLASS I taught was Editorial Design, at the School of Visual Arts in 2003. It was rough for me. I tried to teach those students the way I had been taught. Strict, stern, and no nonsense. A lot of the students dropped my class between the first and second semester.

—

A FEW YEARS LATER, I taught at City College. I had a diverse group of students—different ethnicities, race, age, and ability. They worked hard to get an education. Some would drive taxis at night.

TAKEAWAYS

1
Openly expressing belief in your team encourages them to achieve great things.

2
Perseverence pays off, either with a student or an employee who is struggling.

3
Be open to adjusting your teaching or management style.

I didn't have to do that when I was a student; I realized at this moment that I was privileged. That changed my style of teaching—I wanted to be there for them.

—

WHEN MY STUDENTS feel like they have too much work, I tell them to keep rowing the boat.

—

MY BOXING COACH CAME from the land of Yes. Martin would talk me through it. "No good with the hook. Do it again. Do it again. There you go!" When I was frustrated, he made me feel like he believed in me. I do the same with my teaching.

—

I LOVE HISTORY VERY MUCH, and design history is fascinating—it both shapes and mirrors culture. A lot of students aren't initially interested in it, but I try to make them care. I want them to see that we're all part of a big continuum of time. It's the same reason that Shakespeare is still so interesting; he understood human nature. Humans haven't changed.

—

I SAW A BIG CHANGE in Sophie Naylor, one of my students. She originally had this idea that she was going to work letters into the shape of a skateboard. I let her work through it. That idea eventually grew into a whole book on the history of punk rock. Her work came a long way, because she kept going.

—

AS A TEACHER, I FEEL happiest when I know that I got through to a student: I helped them see and understand something elemental about their own work and their design voice. I gave them the courage to fly creatively. But, they have to meet me halfway and put in the work.

—

I'M STUBBORN. I don't give up.

TAKEAWAYS

A BASKET
OF
KNOWLEDGE
BISCUITS
FOR THE
OFFICE.

When interviewing, act like yourself.

→ Once you get the job, you'll feel like an impostor. It's okay to not have all the answers. Be a student, learn, and you'll pass the test. → Tight budget? Get crafty like you were in art school.

→ Tough boss, teachable moment.

Don't act like 'em. → Do act like you're having fun while presenting, and your audience will have fun too.

→ A well-rounded product stems from a diverse team. → Don't let one bad employee bring down the team.

Make the cut. → Oh, you'll be laid off too, but it's a chance to grow.

→ Good news: You can manifest that dream job (hint: connections).

ACTIVITIES

EXPERT
EMPLOYEE
LEVEL:
UNLOCKED.

▸ **PRESENTATIONS DON'T
HAVE TO SUCK.**   P.100

Let's give your presentation a
pre-flight check before liftoff.

1

Who are you presenting to?
Tough (but essential) question: Why do they care?

2

How many slides are in your deck?
If you had to remove one slides, what would it be?

3

Are there any complex animations?
Can the Wi-Fi connection support them?

4

Do you have a short opening story that will
make the information memorable?

5

Do you have a text prompt on each slide to remind
you of your talking points? Is there too much text?

▸ **NURTURE YOUR
NETWORK.**   P.92

Write down your dream
job. Think big! It doesn't
need to be practical.

I want to:

Who in your network can help
you get there? Keep
adding people if need be.

Person Name

is connected to..

Person Name

who knows...

Person Name

▸ HIRE PEOPLE YOU CAN HANG WITH.   P.106

Before you start interviewing, you should know the type of person you're looking for.

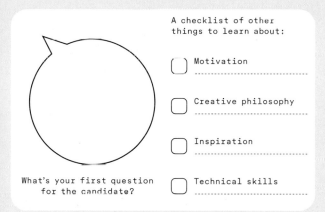

What's your first question for the candidate?

A checklist of other things to learn about:

☐ Motivation
....

☐ Creative philosophy
....

☐ Inspiration
....

☐ Technical skills
....

▸ BE YOURSELF IN AN INTERVIEW.   P.91

Decide the right cultural fit for your next job.

What are you looking for in company culture?

What don't you like about your current company culture?

What can you ask during your interview to learn more?

▸ YOUR A-TEAM NEEDS AN X, A Y, AND A Z.   P.112

Maximize the strength of your A-Team with these four questions.

? What's an upcoming initiative at work?

X Person No.1
....

How does their strength apply to this initiative?

Y Person No.2
....

How can you use this initiative to help this person grow?

Z
....

What kind of person could you use on your team?

Your
Life

CELEBRATE YOUR SUCCESSES, EMBRACE YOUR FAILURES, AND DISCOVER YOUR IMPACT.

▼ YOUR DAY

▼ YOUR PROJECT

43

TRUST
YOUR TEAM.
—
P.126

44

CULTURE IS
YOUR
SUPERPOWER.
—
P.129

45

FEED YOUR
VALUES.
—
P.132

46

ONE-UP
YOURSELF.
—
P.132

47

RECRUIT A
CREATIVE
COPILOT.
—

48

DON'T TAKE
LIFE SO
SERIOUSLY.
—

49

LISTEN.
—
P.138

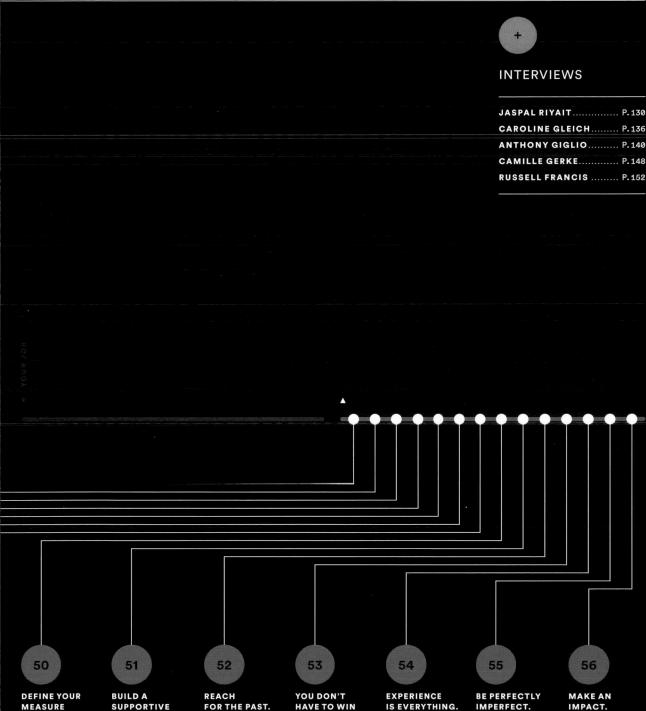

YOUR JOB

| 50 | 51 | 52 | 53 | 54 | 55 | 56 |

DEFINE YOUR MEASURE · BUILD A SUPPORTIVE · REACH FOR THE PAST. · YOU DON'T HAVE TO WIN · EXPERIENCE IS EVERYTHING. · BE PERFECTLY IMPERFECT. · MAKE AN IMPACT.

"If you're not scared, you're

not doing your best work."

—DAVID CURCURITO

▼

P.133

43/Trust Your Team.

Wisdom gained from a first-time leader on a rush project.

 HOW WILL I COMPLETE this redesign of *Men's Health* in only a few weeks? As their newly appointed creative director, the stakes are high. I start working, but then think: *Will my new team feel inspired if I design these pages by myself?* This redesign has the potential to not only revitalize the brand but also reunite a team who's been lacking creative leadership for months.

I delete my redesign file, pull together visual inspiration, and email my team. Fingers crossed.

Two weeks later, on my first day, I meet with my three art directors to review the redesign. The mood is excited but nervous. My art director, Hitomi Sato, paces while rubbing her chin. "Hitomi, what's up?" I ask. "There's no way we can do this in two weeks," she says. Her distress makes it clear the team needs motivation and support.

I work with the team to merge their designs into a coherent whole, and present it to my editor in chief the next day. Creative director success, unlocked: Design, approved. We take home a silver award from the Society of Publication Designers for that issue.

The key to inspiring a team is trust. As a leader, don't burden yourself with hands-on work. Create a supportive environment where your crew feels like they can contribute ideas. Expect amazing things.

UNLOCK YOUR LEADERSHIP POTENTIAL

 DO THIS · **NOT THAT**

✓ PUBLIC PRAISE
Creatives love recognition. This also shows the team how you define great work.

✗ PUBLIC CRITICISM
You don't want the person to feel like they're being flogged. That's discouraging.

✓ REGULARLY MEET
Have a weekly meeting. It connects your team and increases transparency.

✗ ALWAYS MEET
If you don't need it, cancel it. People can always use heads-down time.

✓ AUTONOMY
Allow your team to interact with people in other departments, without you around.

✗ MICROMANAGE
Delegate so you can focus on the big picture. Have your team provide updates.

▼
**Anthony Giglio,
on Parenting**
*"I love what I do and impress upon
my kids the value of a solid work
ethic. If they love what they
do, it won't always feel like work."*

Culture Is Your Superpower.

The value of creating work that would make Mom proud.

HOW DO YOU KEEP THE TORCH OF inspiration burning bright throughout your career? The secret sits deep within your DNA.

Vaishnavi Mahendran draws inspiration from her South Asian culture. While studying at Rhode Island School of Design, she worked with the Sora tribe in East India to digitize their script. She visited and worked remotely with the tribe members, and immersed herself in their handwriting. Mahendran felt the power of design as a force for bringing people together. "No one has ever asked these questions about our alphabet," a tribe member told her. "It was so gratifying. Speaking about it makes me feel emotional," she says.

Now an art director at Apple, Mahendran draws on her unique cultural experience to fuel her creativity. "No one else has the same perspective as I do," she says. "My design superpower is the intersection of my South Asian roots with my experiences living and working in the West."

Mahendran follows a mantra she learned from Ramon Tejada, one of her Rhode Island School of Design professors: "Create work for your mom."

So, how can you stay inspired? Look inward to discover what makes you unique. Draw upon your cultural experience, and make something that Mom would want to tack up on the fridge.

No.

EASY
ENDURANCE
BOOST

**DON'T FORGET
TO BREATHE**
"I catch myself holding my breath while focusing on detailed work," says the illustrator Marion Deuchars. She recommends breathing in slowly for a four count, holding for four, then exhaling for four. From the belly, not the chest. Imagine your breath circulating from your toes to your head for an extra Zen moment.

▼

**Vaishnavi Mahendran,
on the Value of Rest**
*"You can be productive, do the
best work of your life, but keep
it to the nine-to-five of your
day. Work doesn't need to take
over every space in your mind."*

Feed Your Values.

Crashed into a career plateau?
Keep moving to rise.

"GET IT OUT!" BARKED THE expeditor to chef Alex Pirani as he delicately packaged the high-end restaurant's delivery order. "Screw it. I quit," Pirani fired back.

We've all had our "screw it" moments, but most of us don't quit our jobs, especially if we have a comfortable salary and an impressive title. Pirani enjoyed a decade-long career as a chef, but the pandemic disrupted his love of plating food. "I tried hard to make something look nice in a take-out container, but it was like parking a beautiful car in the mud," he says.

Pirani enrolled in University of the Arts to pursue a degree in graphic design. While difficult at first, he ultimately related his new craft to his previous love of plating food. "Restraint is everything. You need to know when to stop," he says.

But a career in graphic design did not provide the same fulfillment for Rui Abreu. "Clients would sarcastically tell us to 'make it amazing,' and we would go back to zero," he says. "They were focused on money and profits. My values didn't match theirs."

Abreu shifted gears to type design. He's now the principal of R Typography, where he has a select few clients, including Montblanc. "I'm calmer now, because I don't want to do everything," he says. "I'm good at doing something unique. And I'm happier because of that." Abreu values being a specialist.

Does your current job bring you joy? Time is your most valuable commodity. Minutes, days, years, decades, hopefully a century—the clock is chipping away at your time. What will you do with it?

BOOST A BLAND JOB

How to make things more exciting while you're still at your current gig.

JOIN BRAINSTORM MEETINGS
They can help you understand how your work fits into the larger picture. You can find new opportunities for collaboration with other departments.

SET UP SKIP-LEVEL MEETINGS
Meet senior leaders, and learn how things operate on a strategic level. This might help you understand some of the problems you face at work.

FIND A MENTOR
They can help you identify your creative goals and solve problems that you may not be comfortable discussing with your manager.

GIVE A PROCESS PRESENTATION
This can help others understand your creative process— it can build a fulfilling sense of trust and community within the workplace.

ATTEND A CONFERENCE
You can connect with other creatives in the community, hear their success stories, and learn how they work. Companies often have a budget for this.

 MY GROWTH PLAN

"I'll persevere."

—

JASPAL RIYAIT CONTINUES TO MOVE IN ORDER TO CHALLENGE HERSELF AS A DESIGNER. SOMETIMES, THAT MEANS STARTING OVER.

OCCUPATION
Art Director,
Apple

LOCATION
Campbell,
California

WHEN I WAS YOUNGER, I was fascinated with the human body. I thought about doing medical book illustrations. Eventually, I got into graphic design, but science plays into my aesthetic. I love grids and organization.

—

I'M SIKH. When I was seven, I moved from Leicester, England, to a small town in Ontario, Canada. I'm a shy introvert, and new spaces terrified me. I despised moving. I was one of the few brown kids. In Ontario, there was a lot of racism, but now I embrace my culture—I support fellow brown creatives. My role is to diversify our artists.

—

WHEN I FELT LIKE I reached the height of my career as a design director in Toronto, I felt like I was working in a bubble. I picked up and move to New York. I had to start from scratch as a designer.

I SHOWED MY PORTFOLIO to Janet Froelich at *The New York Times*. She's very kind and willing to talk to anybody. She looked at my work and said "You're not ready. Not yet." Janet told it like it is. That pushed me to figure out what I was lacking.

—

MAGAZINES ARE SUCH a boys' club, and Janet broke through. She's so inspirational.

—

MY FIRST DAY IN NEW YORK felt like I was in heaven. The most exciting place I've ever been. So many opportunities. Obama was just elected.

—

WHEN I WAS design director at *Martha Stewart Living*, there wasn't training, employee check-ins, or managerial reviews. Managers often fall into these roles. Yet there's no formal education on how to be a successful leader. I grew by watching the successes and mistakes of others.

—

MAYA ANGELOU has a great quote: "People will forget what you said. People will forget what you did. But people will never forget how you made them feel." I apply that philosophy to management. Treat people kindly and good work will happen.

—

I EVENTUALLY LANDED at *The New York Times*. It was a tough nut to crack, but working there taught me to not be afraid of failure. I asked a lot of questions, and didn't need to be the smartest person in the room. I had knowledge to offer and there were people willing to listen.

—

I WORKED ON A SECTION called Smarter Living. When the pandemic hit, service journalism really took off. People wanted to invest more time in their mental and physical health, and they built an entire department to work on that. I was fortunate to be there right from the beginning.

TAKEAWAYS

1

Seek and support fellow creatives from underrepresented groups.

2

Resilience boost: Move on when you get too comfortable at a job. Builds your adaptability.

3

Optimism boost: Figure out a new technique. Builds your confidence for future challenges.

KELLY MCGONIGAL wrote *The Joy of Movement* and developed an exercise for us. We created "The Joy Workout," a video that was one of the most challenging projects I ever worked on. Budget was small, and we didn't have much in-house help. I had never worked on a video before.

—

I TAPPED INTO MY NETWORK. I brought in a friend who's a personal trainer. He coached the model and did the exercises with her. I instructed them to move with the music. This experience taught me how to be a director on set.

—

I REACHED OUT to the photographer Andrew B. Myers. He's really great with motion and takes a quirky approach to his concepts. We wanted this video to be happy and a little goofy.

—

ANDREW ASKED ME for the weirdest stuff, like an animation of a person smiling. I trusted him. He added things in post-production that made this video look expensive. Confetti explodes as the model raises her arms, little balls roll across the screen during the Bounce exercise, and there's even a bobblehead dog in the background.

—

I LOVE WHEN you can look back and say, "Wow, I can't believe I figured that out." I really love working on video now and want to do more of it.

—

I'D LIKE TO take Janet out for coffee. I haven't seen her in a decade. I don't know if she realizes the impact she's had on people's lives.

—

I GREW VERY comfortable in New York. I just moved to San Jose to work at Apple, and I'm currently living in corporate housing, sleeping on a bed that feels like a marshmallow. It's bad. My back hurts. I move to a new place on Monday.

No. **46**

Create great portfolio work by pushing your limits, even if that means throwing a five-foot (1.5-m) wooden logo into the Los Angeles River.

YOURSELF.

↓

"HURLED INTO DIRTY RIVER, Logo Floats Gently Away," read the headline in *The New York Times*. A first in the world of graphic design.

A five-foot (1.5-m)-long *Esquire* logo is tossed to actor Benicio del Toro during his photo shoot. He twirls the wooden letters like a circus carnie. "What do I do with this?" asks del Toro. "I don't know, man. Just chuck it in the LA River," responds David Curcurito, design director of the esteemed men's magazine.

This performative act of design makes sense for *Esquire*, a magazine known for pushing the boundaries in design, photography, and writing. But why should you pull a creative stunt?

Experimentation spurts creative growth. At first, your imagination is boundless. But as you inch toward the midpoint of your career, you must push yourself to continue to grow. "You should always one-up the last thing you did," says Curcurito. "Copying yourself is the worst thing you can do." By taking risks—sometimes outlandish ones—you'll expand your creative potential.

What if you're not in a place where you can recklessly toss aside a $3,000 logo? If you're filming, let your camerawork be shaky. Writing? Try a story composed of final paragraphs. Are you an illustrator? Ask your client to run your sketch as the final product. The worst they can do is say no. Never hurts to ask.

"I'm terrified of what I do," says Curcurito. "But if you're not scared, you're not doing your best work."

▼

Caroline Gleich, on Mountain Expeditions
"You need to trust your partner. Both people need to have a similar risk tolerance and communication style."

YOUR LIFE ● ● ● ● ● ● ●

RECRUIT A CREATIVE COPILOT.

No.

47

How a collaborator can help you steer clear of career burnout.

AS THE T-38 TALON blasts into a blistering speed of 812 mph (1,300 kph), the astronaut Jeanette Epps remains calm and collected in the back seat of the plane. "You need to be completely present for your partner," says Epps about piloting the twin-jet supersonic trainer.

Your career picks up speed: big jobs, big projects, presentations to prep, and lectures to deliver. Try to handle it all on your own, and you'll be stuck in a dogfight. Enlist a creative copilot to boost you through the burnout and give you a fresh perspective on your work.

My battle was to write and design this book, while also piloting a full-time job at *Fast Company*, while also teaching part-time, while also mentoring a younger designer. One of the biggest challenges: The design of the cover. How could *Creative Endurance* feel like *me* but also appeal as a valuable resource for fellow creatives?

I designed close to one hundred cover variations, losing sight of the mission.

Fast Company's design director Alice Alves copiloted me through the challenge. Alves's feedback ranged from the overly positive, "Love the simplicity and graphic nature. I can see it on a bookshelf," to the more direct "Eliminate." Her honesty helped me regain my vision.

"Have a good relationship with your copilot," says Epps. "You do not want to make a mistake in that jet." Whether you're racing at supersonic speed or sitting comfortably in an Aeron chair, burnout is real. A great collaborator will help you achieve your goals with some fuel left.

Don't Take Life So Seriously.

—

I'm designing a frustrating story for *Entertainment Weekly*, and my design director, Amid Capeci, plops into the chair next to me. He's waxing on about the *Larry Sanders Show*, and his passion for the classic comedy breaks my frustration. As I laugh, Capeci gestures at my screen. "What if you flip that?" he says. The layout is fixed. Capeci's light-hearted approach softens my shell, making me permeable to feedback. Problems are easier to solve when seasoned with humor.

No.

48

THE SKI MOUNTAINEER

Q + A

CAROLINE GLEICH WROTE A JOB DESCRIPTION THAT INCLUDES DODGING AVALANCHES AND REPELLING CLIFFS.

LOCATION
Park City,
Utah

▼

CAROLINE GLEICH CARVED OUT HER own trail in life. At just sixteen years old, she set her sights on skiing all ninety lines of Utah's notoriously difficult Wasatch mountains. Despite facing initial skepticism, Gleich spent a decade honing her fitness and ice-climbing skills, and completed a total of 130,000 vertical feet (40,000 m) of skiing for the 2017 film *Follow Through.* "I want to show people that you can do what others think is impossible," she says. "The only person who sets limits on what you can do is yourself." Here's what you can learn from her experience.

How is mountaineering creative? We're predominantly traveling on snow. You have an opportunity to draw your own line up and down the mountain. To figure which way you're going to go. That requires creativity—you're not dependent on established trails. Once I see a photo of a certain mountain, I can't get it out of my head and I become really obsessed with it.

I understand the obsession with a goal. It's like when an artist has a vision of something. I dream about seeing the world from the top of those peaks. Maybe it's because I'm really short (laughs). I just love to be up high and to look down at the world from those viewpoints.

What's a limitation that you face? I feel like I'm an underdog. I'm not the kind of person that people look at and think, Oh, she looks like a mountaineer, you know. I want to show women that you can do what others think is impossible.

How do you get past impostor syndrome? Once I walk out of the door and start moving, I get out of my head. My mind goes into a flow state.

Tell me about a tough climb. I was climbing Everest with my partner. We were around 49,000 feet (15,000 m), about an hour from the North Ridge summit. I just got a horrible feeling that the climb wasn't worth the risk. My half brother was killed in an avalanche when I was fifteen, and he was a mentor to me in the mountains. That really impacted me. So, what I was feeling was a normal emotional response. I was able to reframe it, as a way that we would be honoring and celebrating all of those people who passed away on the mountain.

While hiking, do you imagine yourself at the peak of a mountain? I visualize the camps. That's where you can take in the views—the sunrises and sunsets. But I don't dream about how much your lungs hurt when you're that high up.

What does high altitude feel like? You're really out of it. Depressed. Angry. Giggly. The full roller coaster of emotions. You have to understand that you're operating at like 20 percent of your normal capacity. I train my self-awareness to get through situations like these.

How does one train their self-awareness? You discern the difference between a normal headache, and something much worse. You diagnose the difference between a rational and an irrational fear. A rational fear is an objective hazard—like an avalanche or a rockfall. You have to avoid those.

Sounds frightening. I'm terrified of what I do. But I'm so lucky to have my partner. We have honest conversations, and I go through all of my fears about where everything could go wrong. That helps me move forward.

How did you become interested in climate change? My mom always wanted me to become a politician. I pursued a major in anthropology because I found it fascinating. While interning for the governor's environmental adviser for the state of Utah, I felt like I was on the fast track to become a secretary. I knew I'd have a greater voice if I pursued my passion as a skier and mountaineer because I could use the sport as a catalyst for change.

What kind of trail do you want to leave behind? I want to inspire people to get out and interact with nature. Even if your mountain is just a hill in your backyard or a metaphorical mountain you have to climb. Especially as a woman, I want to set an example of what women are capable of. There's a lot of messaging that I want to be part of my legacy about climate, about being brave and taking action on the climate crisis.

  TAKEAWAYS

1 Gleich was obsessed with mountains as a kid, and it led her to be a mountaineer. What dream can you follow?

2 Develop your self-awareness. Fear of failure? Acknowledge the feeling, talk about it, but don't let it hold you back.

3 Think about the trail you want to leave behind, whether it's inspiring others or creating work that reflects your values.

No.

Listen.

Extract the positive, especially
when it comes from
your high school art teacher.

MR. KOZLOFF, MY HIGH SCHOOL ART TEACHER, SLOWLY HOVERS around our black high-top table like a hawk. He looks down at the gargoyle I'm drawing, smirks, and shakes his crisply gelled helmet of salt-and-pepper hair in disbelief. "You know, Mike, if you stop drawing such stupid shit **(1)**, then you can probably make something of yourself **(2)**," he says. *Listen.* Despite Kozloff's blunt delivery, his words had a profound impact on my life. Growing up in Long Island, New York, criticism like this was a compliment. This was my earliest moment of cognitive reappraisal. "Wait, I can actually make something of myself," was my reaction. I felt as if Kozloff saw potential in a kid who didn't see potential in himself. Unbeknownst to Kozloff, he encouraged me to become a graphic designer, a creative director, a writer, and a professor. ❡ Decades later, I delivered a presentation at Kean University. Afterward, professor Robin Landa shared a few words that were equally as kind: "You should try to write a book." *Listen.* ❡ Words like these are sparks in our lives, and if we fan the flame, they can be torches to carry for years to come. The next time a person pays you a simple compliment, take it seriously. *Listen.*

1

Criticism
Analysis No.1
—
ACTION

Kozloff's comment put the onus on me—a valuable method when providing criticism to your team. **Your move:** If your employee is struggling with a project, suggest creating an alternate version as a noncommittal way to explore new approaches.

2

Criticism
Analysis No.2
—
AMBITION

Kozloff left my course of action open-ended. **Your move:** Give that struggling employee the space to figure out the problem on their own. Guide them, but don't give them the answer. The learning experience will help them improve.

▼

Jay Osgerby, on Creativity
*"We all have a primal urge to create, whether it's gardening or baking.
Creativity is an escape valve for any negativity you're experiencing."*

YOUR LIFE

No.
50

Define Your Measure of Success.

It might involve
a one-way
ticket to Paris and
a swim across
the Seine River.

ARTHUR GERMAIN IS swimming across the 480-mile (733-km) stretch of the Seine River. With a kayak and some provisions tethered to his body, it will take him two months to complete this feat. Every 3 miles (5 km), Germain must measure the amount of pollution his body has been exposed to.

But why? Perhaps Germain wants to prove that he is capable of achieving this enormous feat. Perhaps he wants to prove that he's more than just the son of Paris's mayor, Anne Hidalgo. Regardless, this is Germain's measure of success, an essential tool for endurance.

Your measure of success may not surface immediately. After years of scoring big projects, dream jobs, and prestigious awards, you might find yourself looking for more. Now it's time to define success.

For Sara Lieberman, a writer who is following Germain's swim, her measure of success is to tell "deeper, long-form stories, for places like *The New Yorker*," she says. "People are fascinating—everyone has a story to tell," she says. "Arthur's story is different for me. I don't normally write about health and fitness."

Years prior, Lieberman ditched a full-time job at the *New York Post* to follow a dreamy freelance career in Paris, writing food and travel guides for WeWork, The Infatuation, and *Travel and Leisure*. Over time, Lieberman's measure of success evolved. Now, she wants to tell stories like Germain's. "I love the thrill of the chase," she says.

Chasing success leads you to unexpected places. Once you achieve success, your dream grows. And so do you.

Build a Supportive Community.

No.
51

WHEN DAVID COOPER'S POSITION AT *HEALTH* MAGAZINE WAS ELIMINATED, HE TAPPED INTO THE SOCIETY OF PUBLICATION DESIGNERS FOR SUPPORT. "WE GET STUCK IN OUR BUBBLES," HE SAYS. "BUT WHEN YOU TALK TO SOMEONE ELSE, YOU REALIZE THEY'RE DEALING WITH SIMILAR PROBLEMS."

→ MY GROWTH PLAN

"It's like I'm literally in your mouth!"

—

ANTHONY GIGLIO USES HIS SENSE OF
HUMOR TO STAND OUT FROM
THE BUNCH OF OTHER SOMMELIERS.

OCCUPATION
Sommelier, Writer,
Public Speaker

LOCATION
Jersey City,
New Jersey

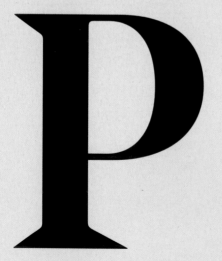

P

PEOPLE THINK I'm an Italian wine expert because of my name. I'm only a Level 1 sommelier. I never took the test to become a master—that wasn't popular thirty years ago. I'm a journalist first.

—

THE EARLY *WINE ENTHUSIAST* articles that I wrote are unreadable. They make me sick. I quoted the Pope and tried to sound like a scholar. I came to terms with the fact that when I wasn't talking about wine, my stories were really funny.

—

MY FAMILY DIDN'T take any of this wine stuff seriously. I wasn't born in Aspen or Napa Valley. I'm from a row house in Jersey City. That approach makes me relatable.

—

IF I'M A BLUE-COLLAR KID that can figure this wine stuff out, anyone can.

PEOPLE ARE EXPERTS of their own palate, but they need my guidance. I talk about wine in a more conversational way. Let's break it down like this: You know how you like your bun toasted, your steak cooked, and your salad dressed. I keep it light on the details. I choose not to geek out over the five subsoils of Germany's Rheingau region—nobody cares unless you're in the wine business.

—

I WROTE RESTAURANT CRITICISM because the casual vocabulary I use for wine writing led to being able to write about anything you taste.

—

I TAKE CLIENTS through the paces of critical tasting, without ever calling it that. I get the first sip over with quickly, because you never know what someone had in their mouth right before.

—

ON THE SECOND SIP, I have them swish it around, then swallow. After that, I talk them through what's happening: "You're salivating, feeling a tingle up the sides of your cheeks, now along the gumline up top, and finally, you feel that little tightening on the roof of your mouth. It's so freaky, right? It's like I'm literally in your mouth!"

—

I LEARNED MY SENSE OF humor from Kevin Zraly, whom I worked for at Windows on the World. He was a funny guy who would gesticulate a lot and tell great jokes. I absorbed everything he did.

—

KEVIN WAS SUPPOSED to speak at the *Food & Wine* Classic in Aspen, but called out two days before because of a family emergency. My friend Christina Grdovic Baltz, who was the associate publisher of *Food & Wine*, asked me: "Can you get onstage in front of 150 people?"

—

OH MY GOD, I thought.

(**TAKEAWAYS**)

1
You don't need to have an expert pedigree to be a success in a field.

2
People love stories. Weave in personal anecdotes to make work more memorable.

3
Humor alleviates tension and makes it easier to learn new information.

RIGHT AFTER I SPOKE, Christina said, "We want you back." This will be my twenty-seventh year at the Food & Wine Classic.

—

PEOPLE UNDERSTAND THINGS better if you tell stories. When I explain wine, I weave in stories about my family; I describe them like we're watching a home movie in Technicolor. I joke about my first sip of alcohol in utero (not recommended), describing my mother's jet black beehive Priscilla Presley hairdo, and the cigarette sitting in her stick holder. Years later, people will reminisce about that photo I showed of her. I've never shown a photo.

—

WHEN I KNOW THAT I've succeeded in connecting and informing people, that gives me great satisfaction. I can see and feel the connection with the audience—especially when we are laughing together, I feel pure joy. It's an endorphin high.

—

I HAVE TACTICS to engage with the crowd. When people aren't paying attention, I'll say, "I'm sorry to pick on you, but are you not into red wine? Are you waiting for the white wine?" Or if someone is speaking when I am, I'll reference my childhood. "I'll ask, 'Do you have a question?'" Then I explain that when I ask if you have a question, that's passive-aggressive Catholic school nun for "why are you speaking when I'm speaking?" People laugh, but they pay attention.

—

I FIND MYSELF AT EVENTS with celebrated, very noteworthy people—chefs, businesspeople, pop stars. It can be intimidating, and I fall into the trap of telling myself that I'm not good enough.

—

MY WIFE BUILDS ME back up. "No one in that room knows as much as you do," she says, "unless it's a Master Sommelier convention, of course."

THE PAST.

↓

A MYSTICAL WHIR OF inspiration was felt in the air when the Duffer Brothers approached design firm Imaginary Forces to create the title sequence for *Stranger Things*. The directing duo referenced type-driven title sequences for movies such as *Alien* and *The Dead Zone*, which was a delight for creative director Michelle Dougherty. "I've always been trying to sell clients on the idea of creating emotion through a typographic solution," she says.

The typographic sequences were originally designed by Richard Greenberg, founder of design firm R/GA, which spun

Could wearing a red dress to the Emmys help you win an award for a hit TV show? *Stranger Things* have occurred.

off into Imaginary Forces. "His design was so innovative—he created a mood through typography," says Dougherty.

Pulling inspiration from the past can propel you forward in your career, whether it's drawing on a creative hero like Greenberg or forgoing technology for a classic creative tool.

At first pass, the *Stranger Things* titles felt too polished, but the designers didn't quit. They shelved contemporary animation software and turned to Kodaliths, a classic photographic film that allowed them to pass light through the negatives. This unconventional

▼

**Anthony Giglio,
on Working Hard**
*"My grandparents had to
prove they were hardworking
members of society. I wouldn't
be as successful if they didn't
give me this gift of grit."*

R O F

R E A C H

process resulted in the eerie, glowy, ruby-red throwback *Stranger Things* look.

The title sequence was a hit, and it exploded in popularity, appearing everywhere from memes, T-shirts, and even a website generating custom *Stranger Things* typography. But then...something especially magical happened. The titles were nominated for an Emmy.

This wasn't Dougherty's first Emmy experience; in years past, she snagged six nominations for shows such as *Boardwalk Empire, Black Sails,* and *Jessica Jones.* Naturally, she was hesitant. Dougherty jokes, "I was like the Susan Lucci of graphic

design: Often nominated, but I never won." As a good luck charm, Dougherty attended the Emmys in a red dress, as an ode to *Stranger Things.* It worked. She won. "I was in shock. It was so exciting for everyone on my team," she says. "Even for Richard Greenberg. He didn't work on this, but his influence was felt."

Uninspired? Reach for the past and hit the books. Discover a creative hero. Apply a classic technique in a new context.

While you may win an award, first place isn't everything. Turn the page and discover how a second-place finish scored a marathoner a lifetime of success.

No. 52

53/You Don't Have to Win an Award.

Finish the Boston Marathon in second place and live a lifetime of success.

DICK BEARDSLEY LEADS the 1982 Boston Marathon, but he can hear the sound of Alberto Salazar's breath as he trails behind. With only ¾ miles (1.2 km) to go, will Beardsley come in first place? Does it *really* matter if he does? In your creative journey, is the goal to win or to strive hard?

"C'mon Richard, you can do it," Beardsley chants to himself. Unfortunately, positive self-talk can't fix the pothole he sinks his right foot into. Salazar snatches the lead and finishes in first place. Two seconds behind Salazar's record-breaking victory, Beardsley finishes in two hours, eight minutes, and fifty-three seconds. At the time, this is the closest second place in the history of the Boston Marathon.

Creative competitions are important: They create goals. But you won't always win. There will be circumstances to blame, like a bad client or budget—your version of the pothole. Reflect on what you learned and how you can continue to develop your skills.

Beardsley's story is a rock-solid example of endurance. Forty years later, he's still optimistic. "I don't think any athlete has gotten more bang for their buck by finishing in second place than I have," he says. He persists as a runner, eventually winning a Guinness World Record for the only man to run thirteen consecutive bests in a marathon.

WHAT TO DO WHEN YOU DON'T WIN

(+) ANALYZE THE COMPETITION
Are there any themes or trends in the winning work? Is this something you'd incorporate into your next project or do the complete opposite of?

(+) HAVE A SENSE OF HUMOR
Judges will pick their favorite work based on a variety of factors, including stylistic preferences, biases, and fatigue over seeing too many entries.

(+) FOCUS ON THE LEARNINGS
Think about the future, not the results of where you are now. What'd you learn, and how can you develop your skills? This is a growth mindset.

(+) DON'T BLAME OTHERS
"Focus on the parts you had control over," says Zakiya Pope, senior behavioral designer-vice president, U.S. Bank. How could you have reacted differently?

▼
**Peter Yang,
on Inspiration**
*"Find the balance by
being inspired by
what's new and sticking
to what you believe in."*

No.

54

HOW TO LEARN
SOMETHING NEW

Experience
is Everything.

The cheat code
to overcoming
the existential
crisis of artificial
intelligence
stealing your job.
Plus: Nintendo!

AN ASTRONAUT STANDS ALONE IN A craggy, desolate landscape. Stars flicker across the pitch-black galaxy. Saturn looms in the distance, and a gargantuan planet hovers over the astronaut, leaving them miniscule in scale. They are not real, none of this is real—in fact, they are composed of thousands of black and white pixels that were generated by a piece of AI software called Midjourney.

Titled "Astral Unknown," this piece of art belongs to the illustrator Michael Brandon Myers. Growing up in the 1980s, Myers loved eight-bit video games. "The visuals were so restricted. Artists had to be creative," he says. Myers put a similar restriction on himself when illustrating "Astral Unknown" by rendering the artwork in a black-and-white pixel style, which harkens back to the days of Nintendo Gameboy.

Playing all those video games as a kid pays off for Myers: The pixel style stands out against the sameness of overly polished AI art.

Back on Earth, it feels like AI is taking over. But you have a defense for your creativity: personal experience. AI can prototype ideas. It can eliminate route tasks. It can source nearly unlimited amounts of information. But AI can't add life experience, the imperfection, the emotion, that infuses life into creative work.

Nintendo was an era of creative discovery in Myers's youth, and the future of AI is a mystery—that led him to the concept of "Astral Unknown." What will you make?

(+)	**SCHEDULE A TIME** —	This will put you in the habit of learning. A realistic chunk of time, like an hour, will allow you to process info without feeling overwhelmed. Learning is tiring!
(+)	**START SMALL** —	Create tangible goals to feel accomplished instead of discouraged. If you're writing, start with two hundred words a day. Eventually, you'll work up to one thousand.
(+)	**BE HUMBLE** —	Share your work with multiple experts for feedback and be open to improvements. Analyze their points of view for similarities and differences.

Be Perfectly Imperfect.

How to establish your creative voice in just three days.

CHICKEN CUTTIES. CAE SAL. SUNDAY Supps. Say *what?* We'll get to that, but first, let's grab a bite to eat with chef Molly Baz.

It's been three days since she quit her writing job at the food magazine *Bon Appétit,* where Baz developed her approachable personality across print and video. How will she establish her creative voice?

Baz sits with a friend to strategize her next move: the launch of a newsletter. "People don't care if the recipes are from Molly at *Bon Appétit,*" her friend says. "They just want you." An empowering moment.

You might worry about being the real You, as fear of rejection and conformity arise. *Will people like*

CARVE OUT YOUR NICHE

EMBRACE THE PAST
Reflect on your unique work experiences and skills. Baz's writing and on-camera experience set her apart.

ENVISION THE FUTURE
Stay attuned to the needs of your target market. Baz bucked the trend of formality in cookbooks with a relatable approach.

you? Will you fit into your industry? Baz's example proves the value of standing out by being imperfect.

To answer my original query, Baz's abbreviations for chicken cutlets, Caesar salad, and Sunday supper strain the stress out of the cooking experience. These casual recipe titles sound like ones your best friend might suggest throwing together as the two of you hang out in the kitchen. "Chicken Cutty" makes the process of brining, breading, and frying a piece of poultry feel achievable, especially for a cook who fumbles his way through the kitchen (that would be me).

Baz's creative voice carved her space in the food world. Her initial Patreon newsletter grows into a cooking club, titled The Club. Two cookbooks, *Cook This Book* and *More in More,* follow, along with a line of cookware for Crate & Barrel.

"I want people to recognize when a dish feels like me," she says. "I don't want it to feel like it could be anything you find on Recipes.com." Your creative voice will help you stand out like this food personality, whose show, *Hit the Kitch,* sports a number of subscribers in the six-figure range on YouTube.

During our interview, I asked about her creative process. "Do you sit down and write a bunch of different recipe names before deciding on one?" I ask.

"No, that's just how I speak," she replies, with utmost confidence. Fair.

No.
55

THE NINE-YEAR-OLD

DISPATCHES FROM EARLY CHILDHOOD, VIA **CAMILLE GERKE.**

LOCATION
Jersey City,
New Jersey

CAMILLE GERKE AND I SIT ON THE floor of her living room, and she's drawing with colored markers. As she explains the strifes of a Thanksgiving art project gone awry at school, she remains fixated on the task at hand: a drawing of aliens and monsters. Her mind is racing. "When I'm angry, I draw because it helps me calm down," she says, her voice matter-of-fact. Within minutes, she's transformed a blank sheet of paper into a canvas full of dreams. I spoke with Gerke to learn how adults can resurrect their childhood imagination.

What can adults learn from kids? Adults worry about work. And work is boring. You need to look at it from a child's perspective. Children's brains are hardwired for imagination and curiosity. As soon as adults take on everyday responsibilities, they forget what their childhood was like.

How would you describe your childhood right now? Good. I have a cat, and I get to walk him. Not many people get to walk their cat.

Do you get any ideas from your cat? Yes. I recently made a book called *The World of Blue* (her cat's name). Blue wakes up. Cleans his bedroom. Then he sits on Camille's face and meows until she's up.

What do you want to be when you grow up? A zookeeper so I could work with Bengal tigers.

I'd also love to make my own TV show. It would be about a high school girl that also fights bad guys by shooting lasers out of her hands. She works for the government, but is trying to keep it a secret. I'd also really love to be an illustrator for a book.

What would stop you from being an illustrator? If someone ripped up all my drawings. That's it.

How long does it take you to finish a drawing? Three minutes. I visualize it in my head first, so I have a better idea of what I want to draw. Right now I'm in a phase where I don't like to color my drawings, so I can do them quicker. I like to hum while I draw. It helps me focus. (Takes out a drawing.) This is about a girl named Alexa. One night a UFO crashes in their backyard. This is Number Twelve. She's from another planet called Bop.

How do you start a drawing? Usually, I have thoughts about the character in my brain. I start with the head shape, add the hair, the eyes, and the nose. If I draw a speech bubble next to them, then I add another character. Otherwise they'd be talking to themselves, and that's just weird.

What are you drawing in school right now? Thanksgiving is soon, so we're making turkeys. It started out really easy because I saw a male turkey, called a Tom, in Pennsylvania, and I put it in my memory box. But then, while I was painting the turkey, I made a huge mistake and totally messed it up. I was using too much water, and the paint smudged. I was so angry! I was fixated on this feather clump. My teacher comforted me and said, "The more you worry, the harder it's going to be for you to finish. You'll focus on the things that are wrong with it, instead of the things that are right with it."

That's great advice. Did it help you? Yes! I started by improving what was wrong with the turkey. I focused on getting rid of each imperfection before moving on to the next. It's just an artist's instinct.

Are there any other classes you like? Writing is fun, and I could do it for hours. But, I spend a lot of time drawing, so I don't write. Also, writing makes my hand really sore.

What else are you drawing in school? I recently entered a contest to make a drawing for the school yearbook. I didn't make any sketches. I drew it in fifteen minutes, and I thought about the diversity of my friends when I drew all of the characters.

What worries you? Grades. They toy with a child's emotions. You could change a child's perspective of school by giving them too much homework. I'm also worried about getting older. I don't want to lose my creativity.

Do you have any final words of advice for adults on how to be more creative? If you don't like your job, then quit it, and do something fun.

TAKEAWAYS

1 Before you start working, take a moment to visualize your creation. Doodle! Don't jump right onto the computer.

2 Mistakes are part of the creative process. Instead of fixating on what's wrong, focus on what's right.

3 Kids don't think practically, and that works to their advantage. Think big when you're brainstorming. You can always dial it back.

YOU'VE LEAPT OVER THE distractions, rolled under the barrage of revisions, and skipped from job to job. The wall that stands before you is a tough one to climb: your midlife crisis. How will you overcome this obstacle?

As a young designer, I had big aspirations of breaking into the publishing industry. I drafted my checklist and chipped away, *literally* working at every single place I dreamed of. *Entertainment Weekly*, check. *Esquire*, check. *Popular Science*, check. *Men's Health*, double-check. *Fast Company*, check.

But now, just like Sara Lieberman, my measure of success has evolved. What's next when you're only two decades into your career? And to make matters worse, the publishing industry is, well, not exactly thriving as it once was. If this were a movie, cut to the scene where I'm running as the ground is collapsing behind me and magazines are falling into the pit. There aren't many left. So...where to next? Midlife crisis: Activated.

The power-up to overcome my midlife crisis was discovered a few blocks away from me in Jersey City.

The deadline was looming for this manuscript. Running on fumes, I took my work to a local coffee shop. Cliché, I know, but I wanted to have the full writerly experience, as this was my first book. Among the sound of coffee beans buzzing and frothing milk gurgling, a gravelly voice emerged. It was an older gentleman, sharing writing advice with a young barista on break.

"Can I read you a poem I once wrote?" he asks, seizing a teachable moment. The poem was about his time during the Vietnam era, aboard a steam-propelled ship. A powerful piece. Both the barista and I felt the weight of the words.

"Damn, that was good," I say, as an icebreaker. His name was Russell Francis.

MAKE AN

Use your creative superpowers for the greater good.

Interviewing a stranger for this book was a bucket-list item of mine, so I mustered the courage to ask Francis to be a part of this project. His wisdom would be perfect. The next day, we have a great conversation, and it becomes clear to me: That interview will be the end of the book.

The day before the manuscript was due, I'm rushing to edit this last-minute interview, and amidst the pangs of uncertainty over the whole project, Francis calls me. *Crap. Is he going to back out?* I worry. "Son, you've got some balls for asking a stranger to be in your book," he says. "But

what you're doing is really special. Creatives need inspiration to keep working."

I made an impact on him, and in return, he made an impact on me. This feeling unlocked an extra gear to drive faster and harder on this book, because I could clearly see the purpose of my craft as a writer. I broke through the wall of my midlife crisis, and I discovered the impact I want to continue to make.

Everyone you've met in this book aspires to make an impact.

There was Molly Baz, who was making cooking more accessible. Jay Osgerby, who was designing objects with a purpose. Dean Karnazes, who was inspiring others to run. Anthony Giglio, who was challenging people's perceptions of wine. And Caroline Gleich, who was breaking down gender barriers in the outdoors.

Reader, now it's your turn. What kind of impact do you want to make? Is it in your culture? Your environment? It can be local, global, or hey, even in outer space. But once you discover your impact, you'll unlock your Creative Endurance.

→ MY GROWTH PLAN

"Don't tell me I can't do something."

—

RUSSELL FRANCIS DISCOVERED HIS CREATIVITY LATER IN LIFE, AND AT SEVENTY-SIX YEARS OLD, WON'T LET GO OF IT.

OCCUPATION
Poet,
Painter

LOCATION
Jersey City,
New Jersey

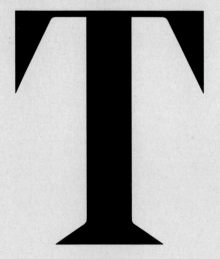

T

THREE YEARS, NINE MONTHS, and twenty-seven days later, when I returned from war, I was not the same person.

—

THE VIETNAM WAR started as I graduated high school in Jersey City. I chose to go into the United States Navy. I wanted to make my father proud.

—

I WAS THE MAIN PROPULSION engineer on an aircraft carrier. I worked in the boiler room, and the engine was in there. Steam propulsion. Very hot.

—

WE WERE IN ASIA, and in the distance, we saw the USS *Liberty* coming toward us. Smoke was pouring out of it, so obviously something was wrong. We had to prepare for an attack. I figured a world war was happening.

I WENT DOWN into the hole. They locked the door behind me, and I had to do my job. Monitor the gauges on the wall. I'm down there, looking at a nuclear device that is damn near going to blow up and destroy everything around me. I had three seconds to shut the entire engine room down, or we'd be done. I was in alert mode.

—

THIS WAS THE EVENT that triggered my PTSD. I was emotionally shattered, but my art was buried deep within.

—

EVENTUALLY, AFTER THE war ended, I was 100 percent disabled. I could no longer work. I didn't want to accept that I was disabled. Don't tell me I can't do something.

—

ALL OF A SUDDEN, I started to write.

—

I SHOWED SOME WRITING to a friend of mine, Pete. "That's good shit," he says.

—

"IF YOU SAY SO," I tell him. I am not educated. High school education. I wanted to go to college, but went into the navy instead. Pete's a bright guy, and I trust him.

—

I WAS WORKING ON A PAINTING. On wood. I brought it outside in front of my house, listening to whatever this creative voice inside of me is. The school day for the children was over, and a few kids walk by. They say, "Hey, Mister, that's really nice."

—

I SHOWED THAT PIECE to Pete too. He says "You're gonna have to do something with this."

—

I WENT TO THE NEWARK School of Fine and Industrial Art to show the artistic director my work. She asks me, "How do you paint?" I didn't

know how to answer. I thought you just wore a beret or something. I said to her, "I put the canvas on the floor. I get on my hands and knees, and I fight with it. It makes me crazy." She says, "You're an artist. That's what artists do."

—

AFTER LOOKING at my paintings, she says, "You are now a matriculated student in the school."

—

THAT WAS THE FIRST TIME I felt like a man that was given something very important.

—

IN 1994, I WENT to the decommissioning ceremony for the ship I was on during the Vietnam era. I'm standing between two guys, and I take a poem out of my pocket. I read it. The guy next to me says, "I had to read that poem in college. I always wanted to meet the writer. Do you know who he is?" I tell him, "Yeah. It's me."

—

THIS WAS MY POEM, "More Steam." It came from the heart. I wrote it in one shot, about that ship I was on, and sent it to the National Library of Poetry. I couldn't wrap my head around the fact that this guy read my poem.

—

IF I COULD PURSUE another creative activity, I would act. I can live the emotions of other characters through what I was denied. I would play Steve McQueen's character in *The Sand Pebbles*.

—

WITHOUT MY MILITARY training, I would not have the discipline to continue to paint, write, and see my creativity unfold.

—

I'M SEVENTY-SIX YEARS OLD. At this point, I need to stay alert. Breath to breath. Moment to moment. I need to be fully available to everything that's happening in my day. Creativity is a gift.

(**TAKEAWAYS**)

1
Sometimes a compliment from a stranger can push you forward.

2
Discipline is required for long-term creativity.

3
It's never too late to explore your creative potential.

TAKEAWAYS

→ Focus on the growth, not the award (but enjoy one when you win!).

→ Just when you think you've crossed the finish line, your goals will evolve. Money isn't everything.

→ Create purposeful work that aligns

with your values. → Give your team autonomy, and they'll make great things. → Find an honest collaborator. → Use your unique life experience as inspiration for innovative ideas. → Be imperfect—you'll stand out. → Break out of your comfort zone for continued growth. → Pick a field, make a change: environment, politics, transportation, whatever. Just be sure you're passionate about it.

 # ACTIVITIES

LIFE'S
(NOT-SO)
TOUGHEST
QUESTIONS,
ANSWERED.

▸ **MAKE AN
IMPACT.**
                                                    P.150

What kind of impact would you
like to make in your career?

?

Social impact

Draw a symbol.

Environmental impact

Draw a symbol.

Business impact

Draw a symbol.

Other type of impact

Draw a symbol.

Why do you want to make that impact?

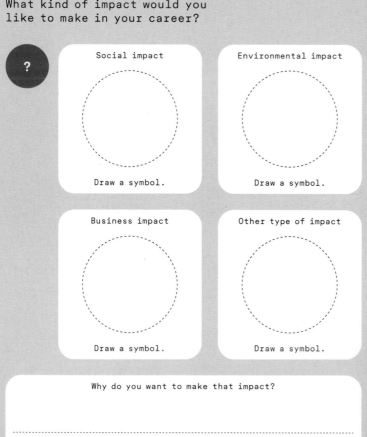

▸ **TRUST YOUR
TEAM.**
                                                    P.126

Write four tasks that you
can delegate to your team.

☐ ....

☐ ....

☐ ....

☐ ....

!

What areas of
personal improvement does that
free up time for?

....

....

....

....

▸ **ONE-UP**
  YOURSELF.   P.132

Let's break your style of
work into these categories.
How can you improve in each?

Strategy

The details

Team support

Innovation

▸ **YOU DON'T HAVE**
  TO WIN AN AWARD.   P.144

Reflect on a time when you entered a creative
competition and you didn't win.

What was the competition?	What did the winners do differently from you?
What did you learn from the experience?	How can you improve?

▸ **DEFINE YOUR**
  MEASURE OF SUCCESS.   P.139

Draw a metaphor for each stage in the evolution
of the measure of your success.

When you started   Five years ago   What's next?

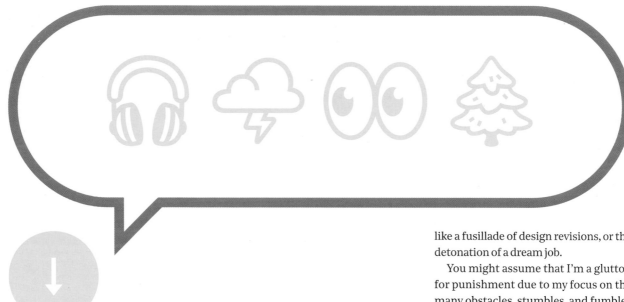

Conclusion

—

"WHY DO YOU RUN?" REPEATEDLY POUNDS in my head like a Tiësto techno beat as my legs drum up the Queensboro Bridge during the agonizing 2022 New York Marathon. This question, often posed by many of my non-runner friends, is a totally logical query for those trying to rationalize the fine art of running in long-ass circles like a man on fire. ¶ Short answer: It's hard. I run because it's hard, and running is a regular reminder that I can overcome hard things, like a fusillade of design revisions, or the detonation of a dream job.

You might assume that I'm a glutton for punishment due to my focus on the many obstacles, stumbles, and fumbles of my career for this book.

Not true. I enjoy an easy breezy day that starts with warm coffee and ends with cold beer. However, I also believe that life's challenges are good—the heat draws out my true character. Through challenge, I grow. And continual growth is my primary motivation: as a designer, as an educator, as a writer.

Each obstacle is nothing more than a mile marker on a lifelong marathon.

When my daily training runs get tough, and the urge to quit whispers in my ear, I distract myself by looking at nature—a device taught by my high school track coach, Mr. Harrison. As I peer around, those trees surrounding me, the ones providing clean air and cool shade, the ones growing slowly and steadily, the ones enduring for decades upon decades, aren't in a race to the top.

Neither am I. I'll get there.

Index

Thank You!

—

SHOUT-OUTS TO EVERYONE WHO HELPED ME CREATE THIS BOOK.

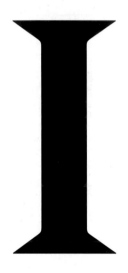

I

IN 2022, I WAS ASKED BY Denise Anderson, a fellow professor at Kean University, to give a presentation on my design work. I didn't want to, but she said it would give me "street cred." Thanks for the nudge, Denise. My presentation, The Runner's Guide to Design, eventually grew into the book that you hold in your hands today. This project wouldn't have occurred without the vision of another Kean professor, **Robin Landa**, who suggested that I write a book based on my presentation. She graciously helped me craft my book proposal, which **Jonathan Simcosky** at Rockport saw potential in.

Once I signed the book deal, I received sage wisdom from Jonathan and the following veteran journalists: **Ben Court**, **David Lidsky**, **Sandra Nygaard**, and **Angela Riechers**. As I sought to fill these pages with interviews, **Michael Easter**, **Amy Laird**, **Suzanne LaBarre**, **Bill Phillips**, **Dean Stattmann** and **Amy Wolff** were integral in helping me find key experts. Along the journey, I shared the experience with my mentors **Stephanie Mehta** and **Brendan Vaughan**, who were nothing but supportive. But it was my first book! And I owe all the steak dinners to **Sean Evans** for giving me a crash course in writing. Halfway through the process, **Hylah Hill**, **Josh Klenert** and **Andrea Nasca** provided invaluable feedback that improved the book 150 percent. My wife **Eve** was supportive of the endless hours I poured into the book, and provided essential criticism. When it came time to cross the finish line, **Kat Kluge** helped me with some laborious production work. Last, and certainly not least, when I was a kid, **Mom** and **Dad** gave me the freedom to draw comics on countless reams of paper, which forged my belief that anything is possible with a little imagination and a lot of hard work.

ABOUT THE AUTHOR
Mike Schnaidt is a graphic designer, educator, writer, and marathoner based in Jersey City, New Jersey. As *Fast Company*'s creative director, he leads a team of art directors and photo editors who create visual content for the brand. He's been in leading design positions at some of the most prestigious publications, including *Men's Health*, *Popular Science*, *Esquire,* and *Entertainment Weekly*. He has taught graphic design at Kean University and University of the Arts, and is the former president of the Society of Publication Designers.